Apostrophe Zen

Further Zen Ramblings from the Internet

Scott Shaw

Buddha Rose Publications

Apostrophe Zen
Copyright © 2015 by Scott Shaw
All Rights Reserved

No part of this book may be reproduced in any manner without the expressed written permission of the publishing company of the author.

Rear cover photograph of Scott Shaw by Hae Won Shin.
Copyright © 2015 All Rights Reserved

First Edition 2015

ISBN 10: 1-877792-85-3
ISBN 13: 9781877792854

Library of Congress Control Number: 2015939943

Printed in the United States of America

10 9 8 7 6 5 4 3 2

APOSTROPHE ZEN

Introduction

Well, here it is, *The Scott Shaw Zen Blog 5.0*, originally presented for your reading pleasure on the World Wide Web. All of the writings presented in this book were written between February and April of 2015.

As was the case with the previously published volumes based upon *The Scott Shaw Zen Blog;* entitled: *Scribbles on the Restroom Wall, The Chronicles: Zen Ramblings from the Internet, Words in the Wind, Zen Mind Life Thoughts,* and *The Zen of Life, Lies, and Aberrant Reality,* this volume is presented exactly as it was viewed on scottshaw.com, with no rewriting, punctuation, or typo corrections. From this, we hope you will receive the original reading experience.

This volume of internet ramblings is presented with the date and time listed as to when each blog was originally posted. Also, the blogs in this volume are presented from last to first. With this, we hope to present a transcendence back through time as opposed to an evolving evolution. In addition, we left out the traditional *Table of Contents* in an attempt to leave this volume with a much more free-flowing reading experience.

Okay, there's the information and the definitions. Read on... We hope you enjoy it. And, be sure to stayed tuned for the ongoing *Scott Shaw Zen Blog* @ scottshaw.com.

Empowerment and the Cost of the Karma
24/April/2015 01:37 PM

Recently, there has been a lot of media attention and television shows devoted to the subject of cyber bullying. We all know the story, someone or some group of people target an individual and then they go on the attack via the internet. The stories have all been told about the results of these actions and the negative effect it can have on a person. Yet, this type of behavior continues to go on.

In all of the media attention and the TV shows it is always brought up that the people who follow this path do so because they can get away with it. They don't have to encounter the person face-to-face and there is little anyone can do about their actions. Thus, the person feels empowered by their attacks and they couldn't care less about the results to the life of the person they go after.

Certainly, those of us who attempt to live a life based upon consciousness and doing good things would never follow the path of cyber bullying. We may love or we may hate a person but we understand that love or hate is a personal decision that we have made and it serves no purpose to vainly attack anyone. But, not everyone is like this. The adolescent and the adults who are locked into an adolescent mindset find enormous stimuli by hiding behind a keyboard or a smartphone and unleashing all of their life dissatisfaction towards another individual. And, from this, in some cases, many other people will join on the bandwagon and take part in the expounding of negativity directed at that individual.

From the principals of consciousness we can all see that this style of behavior is an attempt to feel empowered. But, empowerment based upon stating negative, hurtful things, and directing it towards a specific individual, is based upon a very low level of human consciousness. It is based upon an internal anger in the individual who does not possess the means to get it out in a healthy manner. They are dissatisfied with their own life, they are not fulfilled or else they would be pursing other activities.

This style of behavior is very similar to another phenomena that has been in the news of late, where a group of people descends upon one individual and attempts to beat them up. Having had this happen to me several times in my teens and even once in my mid thirties in Bangkok, I can tell you that with that many people, throwing all those wild punches, it does not hurt that much. You simply have to stay on your feet and keep swinging. It is far more dangerous if you go up against a trained fighter or a savvy street fighter one-on-one than it is to be attacked by a crowd; for the experienced fighter can hurt you in one blow where the fight group is simply trying to get their punches in.

If we look at this style of group orientated physical attack, it is exactly the same as a cyber bully attack. The people who instigate this are too afraid to actually confront a person of equal ability if they have a problem with them. Instead, they hide behind the keyboard. That is simply a coward's way to do anything. I am certain that all of us who try to live a good life would tell this to any person who goes on the cyber attack. But, these people are most likely surrounded with cyber space associates who cheer them on. And, this type of person would not listen even if you could tell them because they are lost in self-hatred, the adrenalin rush, and the false empowerment of unleashing their negative thoughts and ideas that are intended to hurt a person.

But, here's the thing, if you say something bad about a

person, how does that make you any better then them? If you interpret an individual's deeds or actions, with their idea of causing that person pain, (on any level), who made you the expert on that person and gave you the right to interpret anything that they did or did not do? The question that must be asked is, if you try to hurt someone by your words, what does that say about you? What that says is that you are not whole onto yourself. All you are doing is targeting an individual who does not deserve you attention when, instead, you should be doing something positive with your own life, making your self more, so you will lose any feeling of misplaced dissatisfaction and self-hatred.

If you set out to hurt someone what do you think are the ultimate ramifications of that action? Did it make you any better? Did it make the person you focused your attack upon any worse?

What happens next in your life is created by what you do today. What are you going to do next?

Singing for Their Soup
24/April/2015 01:36 PM

It was a cloudy, drizzly morning here in L.A. I hit over to my local Starbucks and was sitting out on the patio in the mist, pretty much solo, as most people don't like this type of weather. Me, I love it.

I was looking out at the ocean and a bird lands on the glass barrier right by my table and he starts puffing up his wings and calling out in his bird-like voice. Then, he jumps on my table. I told him he had to leave and he jumped back up on the glass.

Obviously, he wanted some of my bagel. But, I wasn't going to give him any. You know, in a different time, a different place, a different life, I would have. But, if you start doing that, things just get strange.

Back up on the glass, he puffed up some more, sang out some more, tried to jump on my table some more. Finally, realizing I wasn't going to give him anything, he flew off.

Life is a funny place. We all do what we do to survive. We do what we do to eat. Sometimes it works, sometimes it doesn't. But, we all sing for our soup.

* * *

24/April/2015 01:35 PM

People don't like things that are different from what they already believe or understand.

Names Change
23/April/2015 05:00 PM

I was over in the hood today doing a quick pickup shot for an upcoming film. After I grabbed it I realized I was not far from where I had grown up so I headed over that direction. I actually happened to drive over by my old grammar school so I stopped in front and grabbed a couple of selfies. The funny/interesting thing is, that school has not changed at all. Not in the fifty years since I first went there – it is still the same. Strange... Most everything else in this city has changed drastically.

A side note here... Maybe a year or two back, when the new MySpace model was first launching, a lady friended me. She was apparently a classmate of mine from my grammar school. She wrote, *"Glad to see you made it out."* I thought it was very interesting that she had remembered my name all of these years later. I mean, how many names of your schoolmates from first, second, or third grade do you remember? If you weren't friends, then their name probably faded into the ethos. But, she had to have been for real, for I do not believe that I have ever mentioned (anywhere) what grammar school I actually went to. And, I think I will keep it that way. At least for now. ...I guess if you're the only blonde kid in an ethnic school, people remember.

Anyway, as I drove around, the thing that was very obvious to me was that thought that area is considered a rather sketchy part of the city, the houses were all well maintained and they looked like it could be anywhere U.S.A. The neighborhood looked fine. It looked like anybody could live there. But, could they?

As I drove, I thought back to the '65 Watts Riots and all

the troupe carriers and tanks I saw driving up and down my street. I wish I had a video camera back then, but they weren't invented yet. It was pretty scary. And, there is no doubt that this city will jump off again, sooner-or-later, just like it did in '92. And, would you want to be in that neighborhood when it does?

The funny thing is, just last night I heard on the news, how they are trying to rename, South L.A. First they called it Southcentral, (the name I prefer), now they want to change it again to shed all of the negative stereotypes. When I was growing up there was just L.A., East, L.A., and Hollywood. If you lived in a different city, it was a different city. Like my aunt and cousins live in Pico Riviera, my uncle lived in Woodland Hills. But, L.A., was just L.A. Now, every section of the city seems to have a very specific name. And, there are a lot of them. Koreatown, Thai Town, Rampart, there is even a section of downtown known as South Park. Whenever I am there it makes me smile. Can you imagine if someone asks you where you live and you tell them you live in South Park (i.e. the TV show) they would probably think you were pulling their leg. ☺

Adapt and Readapt
21/April/2015 06:38 PM

I was doing a workout over at my studio today with, dare I say, some of my aging contemporaries. These people forever impress me for they, like I, have been practicing the martial arts longer than most practitioners have been alive. These people really know their stuff and though some of them have gained some weight, lost some of their flexibility, and endurance, they each understand that the key to the martial arts is to adapt and readapt. They work with what they have and they make it work.

You know, there is something really beautiful about a martial artists or a boxer in their prime. The things they can do and the moves they can make are really exquisite. For example, when you watch a boxing match when a great fighter is in his prime, it is pure poetry. This is the same with a highly trained martial arts practitioner who can propel his body into the air and perform a perfectly executed flying kick or opponent throw. But, it is the wise practitioner who understands that the agility of youth does not translate into the person of age. This is not to say that by adapting as age comes upon a person that they cannot produce beautiful movements and techniques. For example, as we reached the portion of the workout today where we met *face-to-face* on the mat, again, I was so impressed with these people. Through their years of training they each know what to do and they know how to do it in their own unique manner. Though their bodies have become older, they have each individually devised ways to make what they do effectively work for them. They do not try to fight as if they were twenty-five, they fight as if they were thirty or forty years past that point. But, from their knowledge, they could easy defeat someone twenty years their junior.

This is the great thing about the true martial artists and here is where the difference between the individual who trains in the traditional martial arts and the individual who is more focused upon the fight comes into play. Whereas the traditional martial artist learns all he can and works with what he has, they never desire to hurt anyone or focus upon defeating anyone, as does the fight-orientated practitioner. The true martial artists never desires to go in for the kill, when there is the opportunity to move the fight in a different direction. They choose to deflect rather than attack.

I have been writing about the martial arts for a long-long time now and this is something I have always discussed, the street is not the same as the training hall. On the streets it is kill or be kill. But, the true martial artist never wants to follow that path, however. They want to be more. They desire to raise their consciousness rather than to raise their fists. And, this is an important distinction to make. As long-term martial artists I believe that most of us walk away from fights rather than to engage in them. For what is the purpose of fighting when we have spent our whole lives training to do just that? We don't need to follow that path for we understand that the martial arts is much more than simply a means to learn how to defeat an opponent.

And, that is what I witnessed again today. As ever-advancing martial artists, the people I worked with have learned and accepted what their body can and cannot do. Then, they have adapted with the times to keep their bodies in shape and their minds focused, and they have done this knowing that a fight is never the answer when a fight does not need to take place. From this, I witness true beauty based upon interactive fighting techniques that were taken to the ultimately level of understanding and used as a means of mental training and not simply that of winning a fight.

* * *

21/April/2015 05:41 PM

The primary reason people do not succeed in life is that they do not repair the damage they have created in their past and they continue to make the same mistakes, creating the same damage, in their present. Thus, all they are left with is life defined by what they have broken not by what they have fixed. From this, any hope of success is held back by the negative events they have set in motion.

How Does Anybody With That Much Ego Survive?
21/April/2015 09:58 AM

From the various media outlets: TV, newspapers, magazines, via the internet, and from wherever else we are frequently allowed to peer into the minds of the famous and the successful, we are bombarded with what is going on with the lives of other people. This trend has especially erupted since the dawn of the paparazzi age and especially since the birth of Reality TV where people are actually paid to put the their life out for display. Sure, some people love the attention. Sure... But, from being forced into viewing the interworkings of these people what really seems strange is how some of these people operate from such a sense of pure ego, how they come to believe that because they are in the public eye they are somehow more than someone, everyone else.

When a sports star rises to the top of his or her game and is rewarded with alidades it is understandable. They have worked very hard and have actually achieved something. This is the same with music and film stars. Yes, their rise to the top may be more about luck than talent but, none-the-less, they have climbed to the top of the mountain – which is something very few can claim to have accomplished. Same with authors. Do you know how many people write articles and books but are not good enough to actually find a publisher? Then, (meaning now), there are the people who have become famous for no good reason. From their fame they obtain riches and possessions, businesses, and all kinds of the stuff like that, and get to live an insanely lavish lifestyle. Though we can question, *"Why?"* None-the-less, they have moved into the central focus of the public eye and people seek out and wonder about what they are doing and why.

Here, at this point, what they say and what they do becomes seen, heard, and analyzed by the world. People talk about this person doing that or that person saying this. But, the question(s) must be raised, *"Who cares what they say?" "Who cares what they do?" "The fact is, everybody who is alive says and does something, so why should we wonder what that particular person is saying or doing, as they have, in fact, accomplished nothing with their life; done nothing great and have imparted no enduring contribution to the ongoing evolution of humanity."*

This whole process is a testament to the culture of now. Think about it, twenty years ago there was no Reality TV. So, why was it invented? The answer is it was a cheap way for producers and production companies to make programming that they could then get sponsors for and thereby make an enormous amount of money. Was it anything true and pure of heart and mind? No, it was just another moneymaking ploy. And, the masses bought into it. Thus, it gave birth to a certain group of people who discuss the people who have accomplished nothing. ...Nothing, but being on a Reality TV show. In fact, many aspire to be on Reality TV. Again, this is simply a statement of the now of our cultural and our time placement in history.

Though some people may gain fame in a particular moment in history, it is only those who make great contribution who are remembered and revered. This being said, much of humanity operates with a limited sense of purpose, thus, they look to others to find a reason to be and they look to others as a means of distraction.

The thing about life is, we have a very small amount of time of that life. What we do is all we have to show for that time. If we base our lives upon focusing on the actions and the doings of others, than that small about of time is wasted, just as if we focus our lives only upon expanding our egos, our possessions, our wealth, and/or doing what we want without first thinking about others.

It is essential to make a clarification here in that there have been many a person who claimed spirituality who has also fallen prey to a life based upon ego and self-promotion. In many ways, all of those televised religious broadcasts are just another form of Reality TV where the preacher is selling his ego and his personality. Thus, these supposed religious figures, (from whatever denomination), hurt many people in the process of them selling their ideas and their ego. This action in itself is perhaps the most reprehensible, as they do what they do under the guise of spirituality. So, it is essential to not necessity seek out the most famous or the most loudly spoken preacher on the block as your shepherd, as they too have most probably fallen prey to the curse of ego.

All this being said, life, as stated, is short. How do you want to live your life? Do you want to live your life in the shadow of someone who has accomplished nothing, yet you make them the false god that you idolize? Or, do you actually want to get out there and do something good with your time and your energy. Do you want to go out there and do for the purpose of doing instead of vegetating to the mind numbing meaningless reality of our _now_?

Other people's egos are fed by you. It is you who gives them the power to live the lavish lifestyle that they live by worshipping at the alter of their whatever-ness. It is also you who can actually go out and do good things. You can move away from your TV, your compute screen, your smart phone, and go out and do something that actually makes a difference; pick up trash, help the homeless, it doesn't matter just get out there and do something that actually needs doing.

What are you going to do with your life? Worship at the alter of someone else's ego or go and make a true contribution to the <u>now</u> of our now?

Maya: The Illusion of Life
20/April/2015 09:28 AM

From the Hindu understanding of life and consciousness it is taught that all of life is Maya. Meaning, all of life is illusion. What we see, what we feel, what we experience; it is not real.

Now, I won't go into the whole intricacies of this philosophy as I have written extensively about it in books and in articles and I am sure you can find tons of information about it out there in cyber space if you desire, what I will say is that this philosophy goes against everything that we, as human beings, have come to believe. For, here we are. We are alive. We think. We feel. Therefore, this all must be real. But, the understanding of Maya can be presented in a much more simple way than its larger metaphysical component and perhaps this is the quickest way to come to understanding its bases in life philosophy.

Let's take a look at people. How many times do people present themselves as something, but once you come to know them you find out that their presentation of them-self was a complete fabrication. What they said they were, they were not. They were only presenting an external image to get people to like them, love them, believe in them, and maybe even give them money.

While on the subject of people, let's look at the truth factor. How many times have you been lied to? People lie all the time, to make themselves look bigger, better, bolder, more accomplished, more rich, more anything. But, no matter what their reason, what they spoke was not the truth. Thus, how did them lying and you believing this lie affect your life, their life, and this greater life-scape as a whole?

Let's shift to a bigger spectrum; business. Do businesses lie about their products, what they can or cannot do, and what they have to offer? Yes, all the time! Just look at the news. How many people are cheated or hurt by businesses all the time? On a larger scale how many businesses hire illegal immigrants simply so they can get cheaper workers? This action is not only illegal but it is a detrimental to the local economy. Do they care? No, or they would not be doing it. We can even go farther up the scale and view historic situation like when the heads of the large tobacco companies were there in front of a federal investigation and they each stated that they did not believe that cigarettes caused cancer. Come on!

Then, there is religion. In times gone past, the goings on inside a church or a faith was hidden from the eyes of the masses forever. Now, through modern technology, some of these elements are being brought to light. And, that is good. But, I think if we think about it we will each understand, just like the on goings of a business, there is so much being hidden and swept under the rung that we (the masses) will never know the truth about the truth of organized religion.

If we look at government – forget about it. There is no transparency, only if the press finds out what they have done. There are so many things that go on at the hands of each government across the globe that most of these actions will never be known. And, many of these actions are designed to hurt other people and other governments. How does that make anything better?

So, these are the facts: people lie, people deceive, people hide the truth. And, they do it so that they can move up the ladder of life. Do the people who know what they are doing even understand or care about the implication of their actions? No, or they would not be doing them.

So, here we find the essence of Maya. Here we see why life is an illusion. We are lied to, we are deceived, we are cheated, and our true choices are taken away from us because we are not presented with the truth.

If we don't know the truth how can we understanding what is truly going on?

Thus, we are left lost to a world defined by illusion.

Who are you? Do you lie? Do you cheat? Do you deceive?

As always, the world begins with you. If you wish to unveil the illusion you must become the source and first unveil yourself and no longer feed into the lie of the illusion.

Life in an Aquarium
17/April/2015 02:43 PM

For any of us who saw the CNN documentary, *Blackfish*, all it did was to state what we already knew, that the Orca Whales, held in captivity, are being abused for the amusement of the masses. This is the same with lions, tigers, and elephants in circuses and any other wild animal that is being held against its will and forced to perform or live in a cage.

The beautiful Orca Whales and dolphins are trapped in a cage, the cage of a very small aquarium, and are completely kept from all that is natural to them physically and psychologically. Then, their captors, like Sea World, try to sell all their bullshit to the public that they are being treated okay and all is well with the world. Thankfully, many of their corporate sponsors have left them in the dust.

The sad thing is, once these glorious creatures are captured and/or are forced breed, they have no way to return to their natural ability to survive in the wild. At best they can be put in large sea pens or reserves where they can, at least, be able to interact with their own kind in some sort of a natural pattern. But, Sea World and many circuses and zoos fight this truth every step of the way and continue to capture and breed new captives so they can make a buck.

Japan still kills whales and dolphins. But, why? They make all kinds of claims about culture, history, and science but there is no justification for what they do. If you ever watch how they trap dolphins in a small cove and beat them to death with clubs, (which I am sure you can find online), you will probably be driven to tears. It is just wrong!

This is the same with the way they stalk and harpoon

whales. *The Sea Shepard* show did a great job of presenting this unnecessary cruelty to the world. But, Japan still finds a reason to do it.

The fact is, we are all responsible. Do you go to attractions like Sea World, the circus, or the zoo? If you do, you are to blame.

Do you eat meat? My suggestion is you go to your nearest stockyard and take a look at the thousands and thousands of cows that are breed and feed only to wait to die. ...To be killed to make your meal.

Sure, it's easy to go to the store or to the drive-through to get your eats on, but who is the one paying the price with their life? If you had to catch an animal and kill it, would you still want to eat it? Instead of simply saying, *"Yes,"* why don't you go out and actually do it and see how it feels. See how it feel to kill and innocent living creature and then skin it and eat it.

Most of you couldn't or wouldn't do it. And, that's a good thing. If you are willing to do it that means you are a murderer. Would you kill your pet dog or cat for a meal?

Sooner or later we all have to stand up for what is right. Sooner or later we all will have to stop people hurting other living creatures. They each are live. They each have emotions and feelings, this has long ago been scientifically proven. Killing them is just like killing a human. Hurting them is just like hurting a human. Stop it! Stop hurting life!

What I Said Was…
17/April/2015 09:15 AM

For some strange reason there is a certain group of people who, for whatever ever reason, quote me. First of all, I am not talking about the people who find inspiration in my (for lack of a better term) spiritual thoughts and put them out there. That's fine! If something helps it helps. If something inspires it inspires. What I am talking about are those people who go out of their way to use my own words to slam me. They do this by taking what I said out of context or snipping a small part of a larger understanding and focusing on a small piece of it. Whenever I hear about someone doing this it kind of makes me feel like reciting the lyric from the NWA song, *"Don't quote me boy cause I ain't said shit."*

These people may take something I said or wrote, turn it around, place their own definition upon it, and use it to their own advantage – whatever that advantage may be. From this, they attempt to paint a picture of me. A picture of what they think I am, what they think about me, or what they want the world to think about me. This never ceases to amaze me. I forever laughingly question, *"Why?"*

Why do people waste their time writing pieces and doing productions about other people? Don't they have anything better to do?

Yes, I have heard about a couple of people who have done their Master's Thesis and one person's Ph.D. Dissertation about *Zen Filmmaking,* where what I have said and what I have done were a big part of their presentation. In those cases, I totally get it. What they did equals something; namely, an advanced university degree. Those people had to write an original paper to complete their studies. All good.

But then, there are those people who want to tear a person's thoughts apart. But, to what end? Do they simply want to project their own beliefs onto what another person is saying? If so, that action seems very disingenuous.

This happens all the time to all kinds of people. I am simply speaking about me because I am me. ☺

People want to project their opinions, their beliefs, and orchestrate the illusion that they know more than the person they are actually speaking about. But, how is that even possible? If the person is living, that person knows what they are doing and to take their ideologies and falsely present them to the world, no matter whether the other people they are presenting them to believe what the narrator is saying or not, is simply a false representation of the truth. And a lie never equals the truth.

So, here's the point... Do you live your life for you and about you? Or, do you live your life based upon what someone else has done or has said? If you live your life by the latter, then you forever make yourself less than the person you quote and/or discuss. For no matter how you frame them; whether you present them in a positive or a negative light, what you are doing is placing them upon a pedestal by making them someone you feel is worthy of discussing. What you are doing is raising that person to an exalted status by making them the focus of what you are doing with your life.

Who do you want your life to be defined by? You or the person or persons you talk about? Simple question. What is your answer?

Six Million Ways To Say the Same Thing
15/April/2015 02:11 PM

I was in my car listening to News Radio a couple of days ago and a commercial comes on. It is this guy stating in essence, *"Remove all of the mental and psychological obstacles that are holding you back. Become the person that you truly want to be – the person you were truly meant to be."*

How many times, by how many people, have statements like that been made? It goes on pretty much every day. It seems there is always someone making these statements.

This is nothing new. It has been going on forever. Certainly, in the modern era, it came to prominence at the hands of people like Norman Vincent Peale, who wrote, among other books, *"The Power of Positive Thinking."* In fact, there was a pretty good biopic made about Peale in 1964 titled, *"One Man's Way,"* where it shows how his teachings went up against the elders of his church and the traditional Christian mindset that was prominent at the time.

Though he claimed his teachings were based upon the bible, they were obviously influenced by other sources. None-the-less, he bottled his ideology and sold it to the world. After him came so many others; from L. Ron Hubbard, to Werner Erhard, Frederick Philip Lenz, who went by the name, Rama, onto Wayne Dyer, Deepak Chopra, and Tony Robbins. Each of these people focused on the fact that so many people are dissatisfied with their life that they took the teachings of those before them, put their own twist on them, and became rich in the process.

Each of these speakers were and are a little different but they all sell the same wares. People are dissatisfied with their life and these people who are dissatisfied have the time and the money to try to buy their way to happiness. From this, many supposed teachers have attempted to follow in the footsteps of these notable proponents of Self-Help and have tried to sell the same thing to the same people simply by putting a new name and title on it; just like the guy in the commercial I heard.

It is no secret that I am against this kind of supposed Self-Help and the teachers who sell it for at best all they do is provide people with a false sense of hope. Now, if a person has lived as a disciple or has spent time in a monastery or ashram, I have a lot more respect for what they are saying. For at least then they have lived the life of that which they are expounding. But, these prominent figures have not, nor have the people who attempt to follow in their footsteps. Mostly, they are simply good talkers that are motivated enough to market and to sell what they think. At least people like Dyer and Chopra have an advanced degree, as did Lenz, but they are not selling what their degree was focused upon. They are selling salvation to a life of dissatisfaction. I just think that's wrong because the majority of the people who delve into these modern teachings emerge no more satisfied with life. Though they may for a time find distraction in the group consciousness or in the simple techniques of fix-it, few will ever claim a new realization and a better life. They will simply fade back into a life based in mediocrity.

Anybody, who talks or writes about human consciousness, myself included, holds his or her own personal philosophy. Me too. Mine is, *"Get Conscious." "Do everything you do consciously."* "Know what you're doing and why." And, "Accept the reality of life that it will never be exactly the way you want it to be."

The fact about life is, each of us is dissatisfied with some element of our life. At different times this may be reflected in different ways. Some people simply come to focus on this fact. That dissatisfaction is all they think about, thus that dissatisfaction become the entire definition of their self.

Is there are cure for this? Yes, STOP IT! You don't have to pay anybody for that truth. Just decide to do it. Think about something else. Do something else. Go outside, meet some new people, have a new experience, and be something other than dissatisfied. That's the simple truth that will stop all of the people from getting rich from your dissatisfaction.

Relationship Interaction
15/April/2015 08:46 AM

Ever since I first began writing about human consciousness, many-many years ago, I have discussed how, to save yourself from unnecessary turmoil, it is quite easy to peer into a person's personality and see warning signs long before they ever present themselves in your relationship with a person. People like to talk about themselves. They like to tell tales about their previous experiences. Though some of these are obviously boastful, especially at the early stages of a relationship, many allow you to truly see into a person's socio-interactive ideologies.

Many people present a smiley and friendly front to the world. Though this is what they present, this is not necessarily who they truly are. Many people live their life from a space of pretend. For whatever psychological reason, they hope to draw people in; whether this is as friends, lovers, clients, or anything else, they present a false face to the world that is not who they truly are.

To quickly see through this false face all you must do is to look and to listen. You must listen to their stories of interaction with other people. Listen to their history. You must see and take note of how they interact with other people that they know. The problem is, at this stage, however, many people surround themselves with people who possess similar psychological deficiencies – people who pretend the same way as they pretend. But, if you take the time to open your mind, look and listen, this too becomes very self-evident.

Many people pass through life oblivious to the truth or to the lies of others. They meet a person, enter into a relationship with that person, and never take the time to mentally investigate who that person truly is. From this, many a relationship, of all types, has gone bad and the person is left with a bad life event or many bad life events, brought about by a person who has spend a lifetime bringing bad events to the lives of other people. For this reason, it is very important that you take the time to step back and truly look and consciously listen to any person you meet at the outset of any interactive relationship.

Our life is lived by whom we live it with. Instead of simply allowing people to come and go in your life, bringing joy or sorrow to your life, consciously choose whom you interact with.

* * *

14/April/2015 09:11 AM

Doing is doing. Done is done. Once something is done it is never undone.

Vision Lost
13/April/2015 03:34 PM

I was filming a couple of scenes for an upcoming movie at one of those traveling carnivals today. You know, the kind with roller coasters and Ferris wheels that you would never go on because they look so rickety. The carnival was closed so it provided me with a very abstract apocalyptic backdrop. Plus, it was located in a junky part of the city. So, it gave me great visuals.

Actually, the title and the idea for this blog came to me last night and then was reinforced today when one of my cameramen saw me taking some still photographs of the attractions and he said to me, *"Damn, I wish I would have brought a camera so I could have captured some stills."*

This is something that I teach my students whenever I teach a class on filmmaking, cinematography, or photography, that you must always have equipment with you. Certainly, in this day and age of smartphones most people always have something to work with. My camera guy had forgotten his at home. It's not like it was back in the day when we used to shoot on 16mm film or take stills with big bulky 35mm cameras. Then, to have equipment with you at the ready, in the state of whatever may happen whenever, was much more difficult. Now, it is easy.

This being said, many people have an artistic vision. Whether that is for the creation of films, photography, art, music, whatever... Few, however, pursue and actualize that vision. Like I always tell my screenwriter friends, in the mind's eye, it is relatively easy to type out a script and have great locations with each word acted out perfectly by the actors, but actually making that happen is much more complicated.

In your mind's eye you can do anything. You can make the perfect movie, take the perfect photograph, paint the perfect painting, play the greatest music, but actually doing it is much different from simply thinking about doing it. The sad thing is, many people have these grand artistic visions, yet do nothing about them. From this, artistic vision is lost and a person leaves nothing to substantiate their time here on earth.

The only suggestion I can make is don't let that happen to you. In this world today, it is so easy to create art and then get your art out there. Forget about making money on it, so few people ever do that. But, you can create and you can get it out there. And, that has forever been my suggestion, get off your butt, stop dreaming about, and go and create art. Don't let your vision be lost.

*   *   *

13/April/2015 09:25 AM

You never have a thought about a person until they make you think about them.

Too Old To Rock n' Roll Too Young To Die
13/April/2015 09:08 AM

If I can borrow the title from the great Jethro Tull song, *"Too Old To Rock n' Roll Too Young To Die."* This is really something that each of us need to think about as we get older.

This whole idea was brought to mind with Madonna Slappin' lips upon Drake at *Coachella* and Drake playing along for a moment but then... A big uck came across his entire being as he wipped his lips off.

Have you even felt that feeling? Old lips on young? Now, some young people dig it and more power to them but very few do. Like I always say, *"Leave the young to the young."* Meaning, if you are old, leave the young alone.

But, there she was, Madonna, a one time major sex symbol. Now, not so much. An old lady trying too hard to hang onto youth and what she once was.

I remember back when we were shooting Roller Blade Seven out in the desert with Karen Black. There we were shooting our tribute to Easy Rider, (one of the greatest films ever made), of which she was a co-star. We were doing the *'shroom* scene at the location that Don and I called, *"The Mushroom Ranch."* Karen and I were walking around, moving, hugging, and doing hallucinogenic things. At one point we are looking eye-to-eye as the cameras rolled and I could see Karen expected me to kiss her. And, due to the angle of the camera, it looks as if I do. It didn't happen. I did not kiss her. We just had our faces very close together.

Here she was, an Academy Award nominated actress, a Golden Globe Winner, a great actress, and a one time beautiful young woman trying to kiss me; expecting me to kiss her. At that time, I was thirty-two, she was fifty something, and this is no slight on her in anyway, as she was a great human being, but I couldn't do it! I just couldn't bring myself to kiss her. Had she locked lips with me the way Madonna did to Drake, I guess I would have been forced to. But, thankfully she did not.

Was it great to work with her. Absolutely! But, I was still youngish, she was old.

As an actor, filmmaker, and as an avid movie watcher, when old meets young on film, it always strikes me as so strange. There are so many films where an old guy gets a really hot young girl, for absolutely no reason. Well... The reason being is that they are a star. But, in real life, it would not happen. Same with Madonna. She's a star but...

We each pass through life. We each live as long as we live. We each do what we do while we are alive. But, the main thing is, with every passing day, we get older; older than those who were born after us.

Leave the young to the young. Let them live their life. Let them be and become who they are. Never force a kiss, it just makes you look bad.

* * *

12/April/2015 09:30 AM

    If you ever find yourself in a bad situation, that bad situation is generally defined by one bad element. Remove that one bad element from the equation and your bad situation has the potential to become a good situation.

Inherent Vice: A Scott Shaw Zen Film?
11/April/2015 08:41 AM

I watched the Paul Thomas Anderson film, *Inherent Vice* on Fios On Demand last night. Now, Anderson is a great filmmaker. He has made some really-really great films. And, Inherent Vice was very good, as well. But, while watching it I could help but to jokingly exclaim several times throughout it, *"Is this a Scott Shaw Zen Film?"* And, *"It makes no sense!"*

I don't know the structure of this film or how it came together. Whether it was script based, improved, or somewhere in between. But, in its presentation it really came off as a Zen Film in terms of its story structure, (or lack there of), how the story evolved, the female nudity, and how the characters interacted, in some cases for little or no reason. It made me think back to a scene I inserted into the Zen Film, *Super Hero Central,* that I had shot with Donald G. Jackson in a car on the Sunset Strip at night shortly before his passing where he exclaims, *"It makes no sense!"* Then, he goes into a ramble of why it makes no sense.

Inherent Vice. Great movie. A Zen Film? I don't know? But, Anderson should have given me a role in it as it was right up my alley. ☺

* * *

11/April/2015 08:40 AM

    We all know what we know when we know it. It's what we don't know when we should have known it that's dangerous.

* * *

10/April/2015 03:50 PM

Once it's done it is too late.

*   *   *

10/April/2015 12:18 PM

It is not for you to decide how you are going to pay back your bad karma – how you will repay the debt for the bad things that you have done. You can become a better person, doing good things, but it is life and destiny that will ultimately decide how your karmic debt it paid.

Big Leagues Small Game
10/April/2015 04:34 AM

We, who live in the *Civilized World*, (and I used the term *Civilized World* somewhat facetiously), commonly forget about how much of the world exists in a state of complete chaos, how much of the world is defined by starvation, war, violence, political and religious domination, and poverty. We, who live outside of those defining factors are allowed to think about how we feel, what is making us feel the way we feel, what we want, who we want, how we want to live and how we can make ourselves feel better. We are allowed to focus on the small things, the selfish things. We do not have to worry about where our next meal is going to come from, if we have water to drink, and/or are we going to be invaded or violated by a powerful force. We get to think about ourselves.

Now, I am not saying that life in the *Civilized World* is not without conflict. There are bad neighborhoods and bad people who do bad things. But, for the most part, life is not dominated by the hands of the gods not allowing us to eat or the actions of political forces or militants who dominate our every move.

Though this is the case, bad actions and experiences do take place around us, in the *Civilized World*, all the time. This is primarily based upon the fact that due to the freedom we experience people are motivated to only think about themselves.

The thing is, these things don't have to happen, yet they do. In the space of civilization these things should not happen, but they do.

There is unnecessary violence. For example, an ideal

example of this is a couple of years ago I was driving down the street, one guy cut off another guy and they literally got of their cars and began to exchange blows. Such a small incident. Yet, they took it to that level. Now, I am sure that most of us, at one point or another, have been driving and somebody did something really stupid and made us really mad. But, we were probably refined enough not to go toe-to-toe with that person over that small incident.

There is also uninstigated person-to-person violence. People want something, they want to do something to someone and they do it, not caring about the life damage that they create. This is the sourcepoint for a lot personal damage to a person's life, caused by the emotions or the desires of another person, here in the *Civilized World*. Not right, but it does happen.

On the larger scale, people get enraged about the actions of the powers that be, which produces riots. The participants destroy the landscape, the homes, businesses, and possessions of the innocent.

The sourcepoint for all of this is the personal freedom that we are promised here in the *Civilized World*. We are told we can have what we want and we can do whatever we want. From this, comes the mindset of not thinking or caring about others and the taking or destroying of the things that people do not own.

I think back to a more amusing incident... Many years ago I lived in this one beach apartment on the lower floor of this building. The way the building was designed is that the lower apartments had these very large patios where the two upper floors did not. They had much smaller balconies. At one point I had this neighbor move in above me. At night, sometimes he would come home drunk and instead of going to the bathroom, he would take a piss on my patio. As I had my bed right by the window, overlooking the ocean, this obviously made me really angry. Other times, when the blowing sand would build up on his balcony, he would sweep it onto my patio leaving sand all over my chairs and table and making a big mess for me to clean up. Though I asked him to stop doing this stuff, and he said he would, he did not. Eventually, I took it to the management but because it wasn't affecting them, they couldn't care less. Eventually, he moved and life returned to normal but that wasn't before he really messed with the life of another person and he did this simply by unconscious, uncaring actions.

The point is, we here in the so-called *Civilized World* rarely think about how our actions affect others. We think only about ourselves, we do what we do, and everyone else be damned. We do this, because this is the freedom we are promised; right?

Though now, I can look back and be amused at that previously described situation, at the time it was not funny at all. It really affected my life.

In each of our lives we encounter situations like this. People who do things that mess with our well-being but do not care. From these small personal conflicts, which really have no bearing on the greater anything, people walk down all kinds of paths that alter their evolution and the evolution of others all the time. Like I previously described, the actions of others cause people to get in fights over being cut off while driving, it causes people to sue people, it causes people to take all kinds of retaliatory actions, but why? What do any of these actions lead to? Does it make the world a better place? Does it save the people starving across the globe? Does it stop the violence that is begin unleashed at the hands of military, religious, or political leaders? No, it does not. All it does is to exaggerate the sense of entitlement and self that dominates the *Civilized World*.

So, here we are. We are civilized, right? We are entitled, right? We live in good place, right? What are we going to do with this privilege? Are we going to think about others, are we going to help others? Or, are we going to think about ourselves?

You know, you can do for you – do what you do and think of no one but you. Or, you can take other people into consideration first, do what you can to help other people first, turn off your emotions and desires and care about other people first, or can you think about yourself.

Your life is created by you. Your life experience is created by you. The life experience of people you interact with is created by you. You are the source. Are you going to be considerate, caring, and giving? Or, is you the only thing that matters? Think about it…

Alterations in the Truth
09/April/2015 07:23 PM

Kind of picking up from my previous blog, have you ever witnessed how a person does something wrong, sets a course of events into motion, and then, not only do they try to deny that the inception of the incident was their fault but they actually try to make people feel sorry for them for encountering any backlash from what they have done? Recently, I have been witnessing this.

If you do something wrong, if you do something that hurts the life of another person, it is really your moral responsibility to do something to fix what you have unleashed. This is how a good person would behave. They would find out that they have hurt someone or done something wrong and then they would go about fixing what they instigated. But, most people are not like this. As an example, all you have to do is watch an episode of COPS and you will very quickly see how everyone lies and denies what they have done. They swear up and down to their god, on the lives of the children, and to everything else that they did not do it when the police officers have them dead to rights. Sure, sure, nobody wants to go to jail. But, then don't do illegal things.

This is the same in life. People do things that hurt other people, but instead of feeling sorry about their actions, they try to turn all of the fault around on the other person. They generally do this via the alteration of the truth. This is just wrong.

Like I continually say in this blog and in my others writings, people are very selfish creatures. But, it doesn't have to be like that. You can be more. You can care. You can turn off your unthinking behavior, you can turn off your selfish behavior, and you can turn off your lying and your denying that you are responsible. You can own your actions and take responsibility for your actions, instead of making things worse by lying to save face while attempting to find some form of misplaced sympathy from those you are lying to. …Sympathy, when you are the one who set the all and the everything into motion.

In life, if you want to live a good life, it is paramount that you care about the other person more than you care about yourself. In life, if you break something you must fix it. No lying, no denying, simply positive action.

You were the one in the wrong and no lying about that fact, no denying your responsibly, will ever change that. Fix what you have broken, don't break it further by deceiving others while you try to run from culpability.

The Truth in the Lie
09/April/2015 07:37 AM

Have you ever had someone tell you a story, tell you about a situation, and you became very upset about the goings on? Have you ever listened to the story and believed every word only to find out later that it was a completely fabricated lie? How did you feel at that point? Were you still angry about what happened, when it did not happen at all? Or, did you become angry with the person for making up the story and telling you the lie in the first place?

There is no formalized code of conduct for how people should and will behave in the life. Though we each have the belief that what a person is telling us is the truth, there is no guarantee that this is what is taking place.

We want to believe that what a person is telling us is what actually happened. We expect for their words to be a true representation of what took place. But, there is no way to actually know that what is being spoken is, in fact, the truth.

Through time and personal contact we may come to understand a person's individualized personality. We may come to understand if they are a person who only speaks the truth or if they are a person who fabricates situations and/or alters the truth of any situation to benefit and fit their needs. But, this fact never changes the truth of a lie that is being told.

Ultimately, the telling of the truth begins with you, just as the believing of the truth begins with you. Do you only tell the truth? Do you alter the truth to benefit yourself and your personal situations? Or, do you flat out lie?

If you alter the truth in any manner then you will never know the truth. As you have spoken a lie, thus, the entire world will become a lie. Once a lie is spoken, then the next and the next and next set of occurrences are based upon that lie. Therefore, you set the entire course of the world in motion and it was based upon untruth.

The truth is pure. A lie is not. Who and what are you?

Whatever God You Believe In
09/April/2015 07:32 AM

There are some people who believe, really believe. And, belief is something that can come to define a person's entire existence. Belief in the power of god, the gods, or the powers of nature can become a person's primary focus. Certainly, when one is young, this is when they are the most fervent in their beliefs but this youthful exuberance can work its way throughout a person's life.

Have you ever met a person who truly believed in what they believed in? I have. Have you ever met a person who was all about what they believed in and, as such, they were very judgmental, telling other people how they should live their life and what they should be doing in accordance with their belief? I have. Have you ever met a person that was a true believer and then you meet up with them again, several years down the road, and questioned them, *"What did your belief system get you? Are you richer, greater, or better?"* I have. In many cases, they were none of the above. In fact, they simply became the shadow of what they proclaimed their belief system would provide them. Yet, they judged and criticized other people while they were proclaiming their faith to the heavens.

Throughout my years I have met many people who truly believed. The Zen Buddhists and the Taoists were the best. They believed in letting go of desire and judging no one. They lived a good life and contributed to the greater whole. Others, however, whether they were Christians, Wiccans, Satanists, or Voodooist, were all about the getting and the getting over; the having and the, I am more than you. .. I am better than you because I believe.

Each of these people proclaimed that what they believed possessed the true power of the universe. They each proclaimed that what they believed was right and what everyone else believed was wrong. Their way was the best way, the only way. But, what did their god give them? At the end of the day, they were the ones who hurt more people than they helped. They were the ones who damaged the lives of others by their ego, their judgments, and their actions. They were the ones who, because of their misguided actions, were left with the least amount of the least.

Let's look at a few examples; Howard Stanton Levey AKA Anton LaVey, founder of the *Church of Satan* and the author of *The Satanic Bible,* went bankrupt. Christian poisonous snake handler and Reality TV show Reverend, Jamie Coots, died from a snakebite. In 2011 a Voodoo priest was asked to perform a ceremony in a Brooklyn apartment, the ceremony went wrong and the building burned down. How many lives did that action damage? There are all those Jihadists in the Middle East right now hurting and killing those of a different sect or a different religion and destroying historic artifacts while they too are being killed. There are all those fake psychics and mediums out there that take money and favors from others, based upon a lie, while their own lives are a complete wreck. I'm not even going to go into all the damage caused by Catholic priests as we have all heard the stories, but you get the point. Those who scream the loudest about their faith are not protected by their faith and/or are not true proponents of their faith. So, where does this leave us?

Belief is a method for you to embrace ego while claiming it to be a pathway to god. Believing is a way for you to make yourself believe that you are more – more than someone else. Believing is a way to make yourself feel superior.

Believing is a way that keeps your from actually working towards what you want by believing that it will somehow magically appear through prayer or magic. Believing is a pathway of destruction because you are setting yourself apart from other people as you judge them to be less than you. Therefore, belief is bad.

Who is your god? What does he do for the person who doesn't believe in him? What does he do for you?

All Because of You
08/April/2015 10:26 AM

Most of our lives are spend doing what we need to do to survive – doing what we need to do to pay the bills, pay the rent, and eat. Though I am certain we all wish it were not that way – that we could simply do whatever it is we really wanted to do; this is not the definition of life. We must <u>do</u> to survive.

In each of our lives, from time-to-time, someone enters and they really come to define that specific period of time. In some cases a person enters and they really do something great for us, they really helps our careers, our opportunities, our overall life outlook, or our entire life in general. It is really great when someone like that enters our life and we really need to be appreciative.

On the other side of the spectrum there are times when someone comes into our life and they complete destroy our everything. Whether they do this consciously or not, on purpose or not, is almost irrelevant for they enter our life space and everything goes downhill. Some people actually do this on purpose. They decide they don't like someone, they decide they have the right to pass judgment on someone, they decide they want to hurt someone, and they go about doing it. If we look at a person like this and their motivations, most of us would conclude that they are very wrong in their actions. But, there are some people who actually revel when one person hurts another person. As wrong as that is, from a moral perspective, that is how they live. Not right. But, that is their thought process.

More common than not, however, is when someone comes into our life and they ruin our everything but claim that they did not do it intentionally. But, the fact of the matter is, though they have not intentionally set out with a preconceived notion to hurt our life, they have, *none-the-less,* done so.

But, how does this occur? Most commonly this style of life destruction occurs when a person simply think about themselves and not others. They may do this because they think they can get away with it. They may do this because they believe what they are doing is more important than to first take other people into consideration before they do what they do. Or, they may do it simply because they are too full of themselves to think about others first. In any case, what comes from this is the same life devastation. Yet, these people may deny their culpability or pretend that they didn't even know what they were doing. But, that is simply a lie to the self. When you do what you do, you know what you are doing. Pretending you didn't know is simply another way of saying, you didn't care or you were too self involved to care.

Whatever the motivation, what happens at the end of the day is the same as someone who sets out to hurt a person intentionally; you have hurt the life of someone else. Then what? What is to come next to them, to you, or to the world on the whole? Some people, in fact, revel in this, they stretch it out, take it to the next level, make it worse. But, at the end of the day, hurting only hurts, damaging only damages, it never makes anything right.

So, this is something we each need to think about as we pass through life. Again, some people don't care, they want to cause damage, they want to hurt, because they feel they have the right to or hurting others makes them feel empowered. People on the path of consciousness, however, are not like that, they want to make every place, every space, and every person they encounter better, not worse. If you don't care about other people first, you are a very selfish, thoughtless individual.

Who are you? How do you want to be thought of and depicted in the annals of time? What are you doing? And, what is your doing, doing to others?

There's Always Problems, That's Just the Way It Is
08/April/2015 10:08 AM

There's always problems, that's just the way it is...

In life, when you do something/anything it is never going to turn out perfectly. It will never occur without some sort of upheaval or some sort of something going on.

If you do, you will need to redo.

Now, I'm not saying that this is right or that this is the way it should be or the way we want it to be, I am simply saying that is the way it is. None of us want it to be like that. We want life to be perfect and pain free. But, generally it is not.

When you do, you have done something. When you do something, you set karma in motion. Due to that fact, your doing equals something done and from this there is going to be the need to refine to make it as good as it can be (at least in your own mind). And later, there will forever be the discovery that what you did was not perfect: there was a mistake; there were mistakes, something not quite right...

Back in the day, every now and then, when you (me) would buy a book, that book would come with a little piece of paper inside stating that there was some typo or some mistake on some specific page. The thing is, had they not brought that to the attention of the reader, that typo may never have been noticed. As books were very expensive to print, reprint, or correct back then, once the plates were made, this is what the publishers deemed was the best way to set all things right with the world. But, did it? I don't know? I like typos. It shakes you out of your mind-mode and makes you think, refocus, and come to deeper understandings about what you are reading. Sure, sure, sometimes they area little annoying; especially in high-flying academic books and stuff like that but it is simply an ideal example of life – illustrating how this is how life is; there are mistakes.

So, when you do, keep this in mind. When you see, read, or watch what others have done, also keep that in mind. Life is not perfect. Life is life. But, the perfect life is like studying an abstract painting... ...And, this is why they are so perfect, because they are not trying to be anything but what they are. They are not trying to imitate to pretend to be anything else. They are simply exiting within their own space of perfection. If you allow you own life to be like this, you are free.

* * *

08/April/2015 10:07 AM

Do you ever take the time to feel yourself walk?

Never Too Late
07/April/2015 09:04 AM

I was in an antique store a couple of days ago. I'm walking around and I hear someone strumming across the strings of a guitar. This, of course, gets my attention so I follow the sound to its source. I walk over and there is a man slowly running his finger across the strings of this one guitar, still in its case. He notices me walking up and says, *"Every guitar has its own soul."*

Wow, now here is a guy that understands. These people are so few and far between.

For any of us who play, we learn very early on, that each guitar possesses its own energy, its own soul. Each guitar not only is created with a soul but it takes on the energy of the person that plays it. This is why when you pick up a guitar for the first time, and if you are in-tune to it; the guitar actually speaks to you. You can actually feel its energy. This is especially the case if it is a guitar that has been owned and played by the same person for a long period of time – when you start to play it, your playing style is actually affected.

Looking at the guitar I could tell it was piece of quality workmanship. The thing was, I never heard of the name on the headstock. Having collected fine instruments since my teen years, stumping me is a hard thing to do. But, this guitar did.

As the man and I spoke, I took the guitar out of its case and studied it. Yes, a fine work of art. But, I had no idea about the maker.

The man asked me if I played. I did. I asked him if he did. He did not. He stated, *"It's too late for me, I'm sixty-two."*

You know, the thing is, maybe once upon a time sixty-two was old. But, not any more. Some people come alive in their sixties. I told the man that it was not too late for him to start playing. But, his mind was made up. He remained unswayed.

This saddened me. A guy who actually understood and actually felt that an instrument has a soul.

It was one of those situations that if I had the resources I would have purchased the guitar for the guy and sent him to lessons. I am certain he could have made beautiful music.

The thing about life is, it is never too late for anything. The only, *"Too late,"* is defined in your own mind. Never let it be too late for you.

Hi8, Digital 8 and the World of Zen Filmmaking
06/April/2015 09:03 AM

As I am sure everyone understands, when creating any movie there are scenes that are filmed that do not make it into the final cut. There are many reasons for this. Maybe the actors flubbed their lines, maybe their was technical problems with the scene, maybe the scene didn't play very well, or maybe there was just too much film and not enough time to fit a particular scene into the allotted time of the movie.

In virtually all of the Zen Films I have created, there have been scenes that did not make it into the final cut. Several years ago I came up with the idea to take all of these scenes and edit them together into one film of their own. I think I'll title it something like, *"Out Takes and Bad Takes."* I finally set aside the time to do just that and sat down to get busy with this project; beginning with my earliest Zen Films first. One big problem occurred, however, my Sony DCR-TRV230 Digital8 Camcorder decided to die. I had just used it a couple of months ago to look at some old footage and it worked fine. But, now... Nothing: gone, dead.

Anyway, on my early films, (the ones shot on video), I used the Hi8 format. I had purchased that camera way back in the way back when, when it first came out. It was great. It could read Hi8 analogue tape and translate it, via firewire, into my Mac. Which was just perfect! This camera allowed me to reedit, for DVD release, several movies from the original footage: movies like *Samurai Vampire Bikers from Hell* and *Samurai Johnny Frankenstein,* as well as to create new movies from the original Hi8 footage: films like, *Interview* and *Frogtown News.* We also had used Hi8 in the early stages of the shoot for the Zen Film, *Max Hell Frog Warrior,* so that camera even allowed me to peer back into that footage. But now, it is gone... RIP my Sony Digi-8.

So, here I am, left with a dead camera that I tossed to the never-never-land of eWaste as they are just too expensive to repair. Now I'm left with no camera to go back into and edit the early Hi8 footage of unused scenes into a film.

So... If any of you out there have a working Hi8 camera or deck or preferably a Digital 8 camera or deck that will read Hi8 analogue tape and want to donate it to the greater good, the larger whole, and become a part of the *Zen Filmmaking* legacy, let me know, 'cause I need one to get into that unused Hi8 footage to make this movie. ...I'll even give you a screen credit and put your name on imdb.com. ☺

Thanks in advance!

*   *   *

06/April/2015 09:02 AM

    When you've got nothing to lose you've got nothing to lose.

What Happens When You Don't Believe in Anything?
05/April/2015 02:31 PM

Recently, there has been a lot of violence unleashed against people of differing faiths. Ever since 911 people have found a new reason to lash out and take the lives of people based solely upon their faith. Certainly, this is nothing new. From the time of the Crusades forward, modern history has been shaped by faith against faith wars. Just last week Somali militants killed one hundred forty-seven students in Nairobi, Kenya. It is said that they went person-to-person and asked them their faith. If they were Muslim they lived, if they were Christians they were killed. Why should what a person believes define if they live or if they die?

Due to modern weaponry and technology people have become very emboldened. Would those Muslim radicals have been able to kill one hundred forty-seven people if they did not enter a university, armed to the teeth, and kill all of those innocent people if they did not enter an atmosphere where the people had no means of defending themselves? Would they have even considered doing what they did if they did not possess advanced firepower? Probably not. In fact, I think we can all agree, what they did was a chump play and those people, or anyone who supports that style of activism, should be ashamed of themselves. What honor is there is killing someone who has no way of defending themselves?

One may argue that all war is based upon a similar premise. And, I agree. Wars rarely begin if the other person or the other unified ideology does not believe they have a chance of emerging victorious. But, that is not the point. The point is, these people entered a place and killed people who had no way to defend themselves, and they did this based upon faith.

But, here's the question, *"What if you don't believe in anything."* What if you are not a Christian, a Muslim, a Buddhism, A Taoist, a Whatever? What then? If someone asks you, *"What is you faith?"* And you answer, *"I have none."* Then what? Of course those radicals would still kill you. But, why? What would be their justification if your answer was, *"I don't believe in anything?"*

I think back to my time with The Sufi Order. One of its leaders stated, *"If a Christian asks you your faith, you reply, I'm a Christian. If a Muslim asks you your faith, you reply, I'm a Muslim,"* and so on. This concept was based upon the fact that many new embodiments of ancient religions teach, the truth is one but the paths are many. As such, as a Sufi, we were to embrace all; be one with all. And, this is fine. Believing in everything good is good. Because at the end of the day, all good is self-evident just as all bad is also self-evident.

But, this is a complicated pathway. Because if you believe, that means you believe in something. If you believe, that means you heard what you believe from someone else and decided to make that belief your own.

Yes, each person has their own individual interpretation of what they take from the greater belief system but belief is belief and it causes each person to do things based upon their belief. This is exactly what happened with the militants in Kenya. They did what they did based upon belief.

Ultimately, people kill because they can kill. Virtually every battle is begun because someone believes they will win. But, if you win, so what? What does it prove? If you win when the other person or persons don't even have a chance at defending themselves, all that makes you is a coward. Mob mentality is coward mentality. Mob belief is coward belief.

Though I am sure what I am saying here will have no effect on the goings-on of the world at large, I think it is something we each must think about. What do you believe in? Why do you believe what you believe? What does your belief cause you to do? And, what if you believe in nothing?

No Outcome
03/April/2015 04:44 PM

This is a reprint from the first Scott Shaw Zen Blog originally posted on 15/Apr/2011 at 3:14 PM.

You know, everybody has a design for their life. They have a vision of where they want to be and what they want to be doing. In most cases, it is somewhere else, doing something else than what they are currently doing.

This is the same with all projects that people undertake; whether it be drawing, painting, writing a poem, a novel, recording a song, making a movie, or repairing a hole in the wall. In their mind's eye they see it completed in some perfect state. But, in reality, it/life rarely ever reaches this level of perfection.

In Zen Tea Making, they spend hours attempting to make the whole process of making a cup of tea a meditation. The goal is to make the perfect cup of tea. But, is the tea made via that process any better than a cup that was produced in a couple of minutes?

I am so frequently bombarded by questions about what someone should do when something they are doing is not turning out the way they had planned. This may be their art, their movie, their book, their relationship, their trip to India, their whatever... They ask me, because people don't listen. I have said it time-and-time again, in so many ways, in so many places, *"If you have expectations, things will never turn out the way you planned."* This is the whole reason I developed *Zen Filmmaking;* because it allows the filmmaking process to become free – free from desires and free from expected outcomes. You get what you get and that is your movie. And, this is the same philosophy that should be applied to life if you wish to be happy.

Because I continue to get questions, let me say this again, *"No desire for a predetermined outcome equals freedom. Freedom equals contentment and happiness. Let go of your desired expectations and you will experience a much better life."*

And I Was the Nice Guy...
03/April/2015 10:30 AM

Do you ever find that you decided to take the high road, be nice, not confront someone about something that they are doing wrong and then they continue to do their bad actions until it truly does damage to your life?

By my nature, my personality, or by my choice I forever attempt to be nice, to give people the benefit of the doubt, believe that their higher self will win out, and that they will not remain in a space of selfishness and/or unthinking inconsideration. As I speak about so often, people are very selfish creatures; few ever think about anyone but themselves: how they are feeling and what they want. This is a true flaw in human behavior and it comes to instigate many a mental and physical battle.

...If people could simply take others into consideration before they make the choices to do what they do in this life, then all life would be better.

Yes, sometimes I am sure we each have met a person who we consider to be very nice. They are thinking, they are caring, and they give instead of take. But, these people are few and far between.

Having danced in spiritual circles for most of my life, one would think that I would have encountered a lot of nice, caring people. To some degree this is true. But, the thing about spirituality is, and this is something that most outsiders do not understand, a spiritual person is oftentimes the most self-serving person around. They are the person who thinks they are something; believes they having something that others do not. From this, they set about on a course of proclaiming to the world, *"I am, you are not. I have something you do not have. I have something I can give you. I am more than you."* Though their ideology may be based in a distorted since of spirituality, it is proclaimed as spirituality *none-the-less.* From this, all that is born is ego driven selfishness – never truth, never enlightenment, never true spiritual essentialness.

As someone who has also made my way through the film game for many-many years, here too I have encounter an enormous amount of people who think of no one but themselves. Many will do whatever it takes to make themselves something more – to live better and all others be damned. The things I have seen and the stories I could tell you…

But, the thing is, all life really comes down to is you. You, in terms of what you do and how you live. Me, I always try to be understanding and forgiving, sometimes to a fault, and this has caused my life and me a lot of unwanted turmoil. I have also known a lot of people who the minute someone gives them any grief they go up and immediately get in their face, ready to kick their ass if need be. I often wonder if that is not a better life strategy for these people put a stop to any nonsense before it progresses to the point where it truly messes with their life. Me, I put off and put off, I believe and believe that the person will wake up; I do this until I can do this no longer, then I explode. And, that is not a good thing for then who knows how long I have let a person get away with their bad behavior and how much of my life time has been damaged by their actions.

So… The point of all this is, you must forever question your own life standards and how you address others in life. Each of us must come to our own conclusion about dealing with others, for, *"Others,"* are the defining factor in each of our lives.

Now, I am not saying that the moment someone gives you grief that you should go and kick their ass. Though, in fact, this method may be the most expedient. But, it may also lead you down a bad road. What I am saying is that you should be willing to kick a person's ass, (and I use that term metaphorically, as there are many ways to counter attack a person other than through physical violence). You should not be like I often am, too forgiving, too understanding, waiting too long while another person's selfish action damages my life.

Define yourself, who you are and how you want to interact with others. Then, train your body and your mind to be able to encounter anyone with confidence and assertiveness whenever you feel your space is being invaded or your life damaged.

* * *

03/April/2015 10:29 AM

Most people want to deny who and what they truly are.

If You Want To Define Yourself By Me...
02/April/2015 08:23 AM

I forever find it curious how some people decide to define themselves by someone else: whom they have met, whom they have seen, whom they have gone out with, whom they had a relationship with, who they love or who they hate.

I forever find it curious how some people are not whole onto themselves. Instead, they define themselves by the interactions that they have had with someone else.

I believe we have all met people like this. The person who forever talks and talks about their past relationship, whether it was bad or good. They discuss the person or persons that they met one time, someplace, somewhere. They take pride in and forever talking about the well-known or successful person that they once had a chance encounter with. Or, they simply forever talk about a person they never met before but either love or hate what they have accomplished.

Here in L.A. there are tons of *Starfuckers;* girls (or guys) who meet a celebrity and have sex with them. Then, they talk and talk about that. I mean come on... A guy is a guy is a guy; he will pretty much have sex with any semi attractive woman. Hooking up with them is no big accomplishment!

All this being said, who are you? Do you define your life by you or by someone else? If you define your life by you, then you have the opportunity to grow, make yourself better, and make a true personal contribution to the world. If you define yourself by someone else, if you continually talk about another person or other people, then you are forever cast into his or her shadow; you will never be whole onto yourself.

Do you talk about other people and your interactions;

your love or your hate for that person or persons? If you do then that person or person is all you will come to be defined by.

Are you, you? Or, are you someone who is only defined by someone else?

End of an Era
01/April/2015 08:20 AM

Sadly, the Jaw of Cinema, Robert Z'Dar passed away at the age of sixty-four.

I first met Z-Man, (as we came to call him), on the set of *Samurai Cop*. It was a strange meeting in that I knew him from A-films like *Tango and Cash* but was surprised to find him on this No-Budget set.

Samurai Cop was a film created by Amir Shervan. Shervan operated out of a junky, cluttered house on Beverly Blvd. in East Hollywood. He had called me in on the film, when I was first getting into the industry, because he didn't like the swordplay in his film and wanted me to make the samurai work look more realistic. He also offered me a roll in the film, as well. The cast was all very nice.

The cinematographer on the film was a man named, Peter Palian. Previously, Palian had been the personal cameraman for the Shah of Iran. But, as history tells us, the Shah was deposed. Peter was one of those interesting people in that he always wore a leather sport coat, a dress shirt with an ascot tie perfectly tucked into his shirt. He had a perfectly trimmed goatee and smoked a pipe. I would periodically bump into him around Hollywood. Nice guy.

On the first day I was on the set, instead of filming we went and had lunch at a burger joint. There is where Z-Man and I sat down and talked. Immediately, I understood he was a great guy!

The problem was, at least in terms of the film, we ate instead of filmed. It was getting late. By the time we got up to steal the hilltop location in Silver Lake, we were losing the light. As the movie was shot on 16mm film, this was problematic. Though I tired to guide Z'Dar in proper samurai sword usage, there wasn't time. Post that, I realized the film was just too clusterfuck for me to be a part of and I didn't return.

Soon after that, Z-Man and I worked together on the film, *Divine Enforcer*. We were the bad guys. We had a big fight scene with a bunch of opponents. It was fun.

After that Z-Man and I would sometimes hang out at places like *The Rainbow* on the Strip in the late hours of the evening, throwing back a few. He would always ask, *"You got any nose candy, Scotty."* The man did like his intoxicants.

Our paths, both as friends and as actors, continued to cross, whether it was on auditions on in films. He, of course, was the lead in *Frogtown II*. There were a lot of problems with that film. Not the least of which was the director, my *Zen Filmmaking* buddy, Donald G. Jackson. Sometimes he would get in a mood and treat the actors and crew very badly. This, when the fault was actually always with him. At one point Z-Man took his *Texas Rocket Ranger* helmet and threw it at Don.

Things also went sideways on my film, *The Rock n' Roll Cops,* where Don was the executive producer and the cinematographer. This event is discussed in an article written about the film that made it into my book, *Zen Filmmaking*. To tell the story, Don was in a mood. He apparently knew he was going to be an asshole and hired a professional bodyguard to go out with us. There we were on the roof of a parking structure in Burbank, stealing the location. We had a lot of people with us, most of us with loaded guns. So, this was no joke and the vibes, due to Don's behavior, were very tense. He was yelling and screaming at the second cameraman, just treating him like shit. I asked the guy why he didn't leave. But, he wanted to be the, "Better man," as he put it. At one point Don starts screaming at Z-Man. *"I wish we could get a decent fucking actor on this set."* Z'Dar, always the gentleman, simply replies, *"I take exception with that, Donny."*

And, this is the thing, Z-Man was a great actor. I think some people never understood that, all they defined him by was his face. But, he was a really good actor!

He was also the consummate professional. He could have kicked Don's ass and I would not have stepped in. I doubt that Don's paid-for bodyguard would have helped either as he got freaked out by all that was going on and eventually bailed. But, Z-man worked with us until the early morning hours of dawn, when he finally got paid his $300.00 and went home.

You can see Don's obsessional camera work and Z-Man doing and redoing this one scene over and over again in the Zen Documentary, *Cinematografia Obsesion,* if you want to. Even after all this he remained friends with Don. I remember Z-man calling Don when he was in the last days of his life at U.C.L.A. Medical Center. Don apologized to him. Z-man told him not to worry about it.

Z-Man certainly etched his name into the world of Cult Cinema. I believe had he walked a slightly different path he could have maintained a career in the high budget market. But, he went astray of SAG. I don't know if he ever resolved that problem. The thing is, SAG, now SAG/Aftra, controls the mainstream industry. If you are not a part of it, you cannot work. As they are a union, they do not let their actors work in nonunion films. Yes, one can follow the path of Financial Core status, but that is only limited SAG membership and there are many detriments to that status. Z'Dar got caught working nonunion. SAG, if they find this out, expect you to pay all the money you earned on any film to them, plus a fine. The last I heard Z-man never paid that. But, he did have a wide spanning career.

Z-Man eventually moved back to his home in the Chicago area. He had inherited his mother's house. While in L.A., he, as many actors do, spent much of his time near penniless and couch surfing. Surprisingly, it was once he returned to the Midwest that he began to get tons and tons of work. I remember Joe Estevez telling me one time, *"He owns that town."*

I believe with the passing of Z'Dar it again signals the ending of an era. I wrote about this maybe a year or so ago when I discussed the fact that no new Scream Queen were moving to center stage to take over for the aging girls of the previous era. This too is the case with Z'Dar. It is a signal. And, I guess that's life, times and trends move on.

I look to the filmmaking that is going on, and yes there are tons of movies being made. But, few are following the path of true Cult Cinema. Some are imitation of, some are just bad movies, but few illustrate the market that Z-Man was one of the Kings of.

There are so many stories I could tell about Z-Man. But, I will leave it at this. You will be missed, Bobby. You were one of the greatest actors I have ever met and had the pleasure of working with.

Locals Only
31/March/2015 01:51 PM

There was an ideology that grew out of 1950s, 1960s, and 1970s Surf Culture called, *"Locals Only."* Basically, it meant that the locals from a specific beach area did not want others to come to their area and surf their waves. One would think that surfers from various communities could unite under the banner of surfing but it wasn't like that. In fact, this ideology grew and grew. Certain groups of people truly came to claim specific beaches as their own. Many a fight broke out due to this ideology.

Even in the 1980s when I lived at this one beachside apartment in Redondo Beach, a group of Samoan-Americans opened up a surf shop and decided that this one semi-private beach was theirs. If anyone wanted to surf it they had to ride their surfboards or suffer the consequences. A lot of violence came from that. Eventually, due to their illegal activity, the shop was closed and several of them ended up in jail. But, that was simply an ideal example of *Locals Only* culture.

Me too... I hate the tourist that come to my area, jam the streets, behave badly, and don't care about the trash and destruction that they leave behind. Don't you feel the same way?

There is a certain ethnocentricity in most of us. We want our space to be our space. We hate it when it is invaded.

The *Locals Only* mentality is much more than something based in Surf Culture, however. It stretches out across our individual cultures. For anyone who has traveled extensively and can speak the language, it is very quickly evident that in any homogeneous culture, be it Japanese, Korean Chinese,

Filipino, Saudi, Indian, Mexican, American, you name it; a person from a specific region of that country will have demeaning feelings towards people from other parts of that country. Though they may be of the same racial stock that does not mean that they do not form judgments about people from other regions. Think about it. Do you feel that way?

This is based in a very simple fact, for each region of a country, people are raised to behave in a specific manner. Though this, of course, is a stereotype, none-the-less, stereotypes are defined for a reason. A specific person from a specific region is educated to behave in a specific manner. For example, look at the United States, the urban dwellers from the East Coast are understood to be rude, loud, and aggressive, those from the South or the Midwest are seen to be red necks, in the West people are deemed to be overly laid back and spaced out. Though these are all broad generalizations, if you look to the human culture for each of these geographic locations, on the whole, these definitions are fairly accurate.

Moving outside of specific peoples born to a specific country, now add to that large numbers of people from a different culture moving into a new country; their culture, their ways of understanding, their accepted behaviors are completely different. Thus, they bring their culture into their new locations and rapidly penetrate the accepted culture of a country, state, city, town, or specific region of a city. From this, new understandings about the cultures of man may be revealed and it eventually may be assimilated, but it also causes friction. The new peoples behavior in the manner they came to understand was correct. But, their definition of correct or acceptable may be very different from that of where they have arrived. Thus, they cause conflict and give rise to the *Locals Only* mentality.

In the U.S., we are schooled to accept other cultures. But, this is far more an act of philosophy than practicality. We too look down on other cultures. Though many of us try to be more forgiving and understanding but when someone moves into our space and causes a disruption to our space, by exhibiting a lack of respect, this is what sets conflict into motion. Whether this conflict be small, person-to-person, or a large war, it is set in motion by the *Locals Only* mentality. *"This is my space, not yours."*

For those of us who have traveled or for those of you who will travel, for those who may move to new areas, it is essentially important to enter any new place in the mode of silence and stealth. I cannot tell you how many Americans I have seen making fools of themselves across the world, poking fun at or simply dismissing local culture. This is why I never associate with Westerns across the globe and this is why they are so often looked down upon by various cultures. I can also not tell you how many rude Americans I have encountered in America who just bulldoze their way into any new environment they arrive in and ruin the everything of the everything.

If you go somewhere else, somewhere/anywhere new, you need to not cause a commotion when you arrive, for a commotion only instigates conflict.

The most essential element to this equation is you. For it is you who behaves in a certain manner whenever you enter a new space. It is you who sets the stage for how you will be accepted and the impact you may unleash. It is also you who decides how to behave when you encounter a new and different culture, be it from within your own country or from somewhere across the globe.

Locals Only?

*   *   *

31/March/2015 01:51 PM

What are you doing with your time?

The Jinx of Going Clear
31/March/2015 10:53 AM

Are you ever in a store or someplace like that and you hear a person saying something, you look over, and they are talking to themselves? I believe that is the first sign of pending insanity. Drifting slowly into mental illness. Normal people don't talk to themselves! At least not out loud.

The final scene in the documentary about Robert Durst, *The Jinx,* concludes with him rambling to himself in the bathroom while his mic was still on about killing them all. Personally, I find it hard to believe that the soundman and the filmmakers did not hear that sound bite immediately. They claimed they discovered it much later, which is what took them so long to turn it over to the police. Turn it over just before the release of the doc. But, that's show business, everybody lies. I guess we will never really know the truth.

Not being from New York, I never even heard of Durst or his family before that documentary. But, it was an interesting piece of filmmaking. From a legal perspective, I doubt that his ramblings, at the end of it, will hold much weight in court, though the other evidence the documentarians turned up may.

Going Clear was another very well produced documentary, though it was presented from a very slanted point of view. But, that's how may a doc is made.

Personally, I have never consciously interacted with a Scientologist. But, being in the Hollywood game I am sure I have met and worked with a lot of them. But, the subject never came up. I was very close with this one girl back in my later teen years. We danced around eastern spirituality together.

She eventually got into Scientology and I never heard from her again. But, I guess that's what Scientologists are supposed to do, separate themselves from everyone who is NOT.

Kind of like the Hare Krishnas, Scientologists used to be everywhere around L.A. If you walked down Hollywood Blvd. they would be hitting you up. If you were waiting in line for the movies in Westwood they would be there passing out their stuff. Awh life and the desire for the better and the more... And, those who are the disciples believing there are changing the world by spreading the gospel.

Though I was never drawn to Scientology, being who I am I did read the original *Dianetics* book and other works by Hubbard – his Scientology stuff, not his Pulp Fiction or Sci-Fi. I also read the book co-authored by his son, L. Ron Hubbard, *Messiah or Madman,* back when it was first released. All good reads. So, I knew about everything they discussed in the doc as it has all already been pretty much declared. But, it was still a good watch.

One thing that kind of struck me as funny was how they rip on Scientology's creation theory. And, the Scientology episode of *South Park* did that, as well. Funny episode. Sure, it is pretty abstract and comic book. But, I think most Westerns who have grown up with Christianity never step back and take a look at the stories told by that religion. Think about it like you never heard it before, it too would be pretty much comic book.

The doc also rips on Scientology's tax-free status. Think how many other religions and religious groups are tax-free. A lot of bad shit goes in within them, as well. Take a look at all the things that the Catholic priests have done. Not good! So, either make them all pay taxes or who cares?

In the doc some former members complained about working for pennies. I guess these people never trained in the martial arts. Me, I taught for this one guy for years upon years upon year and never got paid a dime. And, that is very common in the martial arts. The thing is, if you don't want to do something, don't do it. Life is that simple. But, if you do decide to do something, don't complain about it. It was your own fault for making that choice.

Anyway, those are two good docs from HBO that have come out over the past couple months. Watch 'em is you have the chance.

Black Hawk Down
28/March/2015 08:53 AM

Over the past eight or nine months there has been a few stations on FiOS that have been playing the movie, *Black Hawk Down* over and over again. So, whenever I'm flipping channels and/or there isn't anything else to watch I catch bits and pieces of it. I am sure in the past months I have also actually sat down and watch the whole movie from start to finish, as well.

Hands down, this is one of the best movies ever made. Not just one of the best, if not the best, war films ever made, but in terms of overall movie making this film is unparalleled. Ever since I saw it in the theaters, when it was first released, I was simply amazed how Riddle Scott achieved what he did with this film. I mean, the amount of coordination between the helicopters, the movement and interaction between large numbers of people in the air and on the ground, not to mention the movement of animals, people, cars, and the cinematography is exceptional. This is just a great movie!

Sadly, Riddle Scott's brother Tony Scott, also an exceptional filmmaker, took his own life by jumping from a bridge not far from where I live. No one may ever know the reason why, but that was his choice and this is a choice we each have the right to exercise if we need to. But, gone is a great man who also made great films.

But, back to the point... The reason I write this is that whether you are a filmmaker or just a film viewer, you really need to see this movie. I truly cannot even conceive how Scott did what he did, watch for the subtleties, you will be amazed. Though he has long been one of my favorite directors and he has made films since this movie, this one is a pinnacle of exceptional filmmaking.

Your Words Don't Impress Me
27/March/2015 04:01 PM

Have you ever met one of those people who talks and talks, telling everyone how they should live their life, giving advice even when it is not asked for? I have...

Have you ever met one of those people that the minute you meet them they begin to go into a whole discourse, telling you their complete autobiography: all the great things they have accomplished, and all of the great plans they have for their future? I have.

Have you ever met a person who just talks and talks the moment they get around people, and because you are a polite person you hold back the urge to scream, *"Shut the fuck up!"* I have.

There are so many people out there who want to tell everybody else how to live. There are so many people out there who want to sing their own praises. ...Sing them, because nobody else is singing them. And, here's the point, if someone is whole onto themselves, if someone is actually accomplished, they do not need to tell any one any thing, they do not need to be the one talking about themselves because what they understand, what they think about what and why, what they have accomplished, is already known.

Moreover, look to the lives of the people who talk, for if you have the opportunity to see who they really are, you will find a life in ruin, a life defined by failure not by success, a life define by the damaging of others, not by the helping of others. For if they were what they claimed to be, if they were a true knower, they would know that they would not need to try to impress anyone else with what they have to say.

Therefore, the talkers are never the knowers. The talkers are just the talkers.

Your life is not defined by what you say. Your life is defined by what you have done.

*   *   *

27/March/2015 03:59 PM

If you make the choice to be something/anything you are responsible for the repercussions.

* * *

27/March/2015 03:59 PM

Good is good but better is better.

*   *   *

27/March/2015 03:58 PM

    Does a fraud know that they are a fraud?

    Can a fraud ever stop being a fraud?

* * *

27/March/2015 08:52 AM

Bad makes a person bad.

Bad environment,
Bad people,
Bad experiences
all make a person behave badly.

Hollywood
26/March/2015 03:55 PM

I was up in Hollywood today doing a wardrobe fitting for a commercial I will be doing in about a week. Afterwards I decided to hit over to this one gallery, to see what was new and interesting in the world of art. As I drove down Sunset, I looked up Hobart to the apartment building I lived in when I was growing up. I saw the Observatory up on the hill.

It's kind of funny, I guess. We lived on the third floor in the back of the building and we had a patio. From our patio you could see the Observatory but I never really thought about it much back then. It was just there.

When I was in Junior High my friend Peter (who passed away almost twenty years ago) and I would push our bikes up those steep trails to the top of Mount Hollywood and then ride them down full speed past the Observatory. Crazy... Crazy that we never got hurt, as this was long before they developed the Mountain or ATB Bikes that are available today. I used to sleep out on that patio at night sometimes. Back then, the car noise, the sirens, and the police helicopters didn't bother me that much. Now, I hate noise. It drives me nuts.

Bukowski used to live about a block and half from me, across Sunset and down around the next corner. Back then, I never knew he was to become the literary genius that he became. I just thought he was the guy who wrote sex stories for *The Free Press*. ...Which a few of them actually became chapters in his books.

As I drove a bit further down Sunset I passed the hospitable that I was born in, which in now a gigantic Scientology center. That fact always strikes me as weird.

I hit the gallery then went and caught a brau with a few friends up at *Yee Rustic Inn.* On my way back through Hollywood I took Hollywood Blvd. to get onto the freeway. I passed this one street where gone is the last great coffee house that remained from the 50s, a place called *Déjà Vu.* My friends from the Sufi Order and I use to meet there in the late night, drink apple cider, discuss spiritually, and play chess until the early hours of the morning. While most of high school classmates were in bed, I was there. Which is probably one of the reasons I was such a bad student.

I drove a little further and, again, I passed my old street. This time from the other side. I looked around, as I always do; I studied the structures, I studied the people walking down the street, I studied the city. Though Hollywood has changed a lot – there are a lot of new buildings and new businesses but there is one thing that is absolutely for sure, it is still just a dirty, dangerous city promising dreams that no one will ever find.

Hospitalized
25/March/2015 02:37 PM

Sadly, it was just revealed that reporter Lara Logan had to be hospitalized again due to ongoing problems brought about by the severe sexual assault she suffered at the hands of male protestors in Egypt. When this first happened, four years ago, I was writing the first Scott Shaw Zen Blog, which eventually became the book, *Scribbles on the Restroom Wall.* I was so upset by what had happened to her I could not even write (or do anything else) for over a week.

I do not know Lara Logan or really know anything about her. But, I have spent quite a lot of time in Egypt and I do know about the horrible and violent conditions that many of the women there are subject to. And, it is just wrong.

I imagine I told this story in the original blog that I finally wrote on this subject, but this story is very telling of what goes on in Egypt. In fact, let me tell (or re-tell) two stories.

On one of my first trips to Egypt I sat on the plane next to two female college students who had been on one of those extended stay study abroad in Africa things. They wanted to see the pyramids before they went home. By the time we got into Cairo it was already dusk but they only had that one-day and seeing the pyramids was a must. I, of course, went with them.

By the time we arrived, it was already night. Once there, these two late-teenage boys came up to us and offered us camel and horse rides to the pyramid. The girls accepted.

We went, did what we did, and then the boys invited us to their home. My first thought was, *"This is pretty sketchy."* But, the girls wanted to go. We got there, they offered us tea. ...Tea that we did not see them make. Though I was only about twenty-five at the time, I knew never to drink anything that anyone gives you when you do not know the person and are not in familiar circumstances. The girls drank the tea. I did not. Soon after that, they both became very woozy.

Now, I won't go into what happened next, but I will say that the girls emerged unscathed. No one was going to get hurt on my watch. The boys and their friends... Well, I'll just let it go at that.

Another time I had an early evening flight out of Cairo. I didn't really have anything I wanted to do so I went to the Cairo Zoo to kill some time. It was during the week and there was virtually no one there. I did notice a group of teenage boys walking around, however.

As I walked around, looking at the animals, I came upon them in the distance. Two of the boys were about to get into a fight. One was much taller than the other one, obviously older. They faced off and the first thing the large one does is to kick the smaller guy in the knee. The boy went down.

Now, teenage boys fight all the time, but what happened next really stunned me. The one smaller boy was crying and grabbing his knee on the ground. The larger boy grabbed him, flipped him over and he beginning to pull down his pants. The other boys cheering him on.

Teenage boys get into fights all of the time. But, a fight, win or lose, does not end in sodomy.

The boys didn't see me so I loudly whistled at them and yelled, *"Hey."* The larger boy, pulling down his own pants at this point stopped, looked at me, pulled his pants back up. The other boy rolled over, stumbled to his feet, and pulls his own pants up. The crew walks off with the one boy staggering on his injured knee, possibly and quite probably damaged for life.

This is what goes on in Egypt. Though bad shit goes on all over the world, all the time, what I have just described and what happened to Lara Logan is commonplace in Egypt. That behavior is simply so wrong it is not even funny. But, it is what so many women, and young boys, must endure all the time in that country.

It is truly sad. And, something really needs to be done about that. What kind of a person, what kind of people, would even think about doing what they did to Lara Logan. Just sad. Just wrong. This world needs to be made a better place.

Playing In Your Own Playground
25/March/2015 10:30 AM

I often discuss the fact that, *"You can only play in your own playground."* Meaning, you can only be safe, secure, and have some semblance of suchness if you are doing what you do surrounded by a supportive network of people in a safe, conscious, and creative environment. The vast wide internet is certainly not that.

People, who enter cyberspace, hope and believe that it will be a place where they dance around, have fun, maybe learn some new things, meet some new people, and find some new entertainment. All-good, until it goes All-bad which it can easily do.

Have you ever noticed that on some sites there are some people who are king (or queen)? Why is that? Did it just happen? Maybe, but probably not. That person either is a cohort with the site owner or they contribute so much to the site's operations and/or appeal that they are found to be elemental to its ongoing growth and potential. So, they are promoted to a position of authority and dominance. Or, some people just battle and battle, taking control over pages on sites like Wikipedia. They are willing to fight their fight; oftentimes using hidden knowledgeable and underhanded methods, until anyone who opposes them is either banned from the site or gives up and says, *"Fuck it."*

Again, not your playground. So, if you play in it be weary.

This concept also stretches out to life. Where you live, where you go, what you do should all be safe, supportive, and give birth to the betterment of you. But, it is not like that.

Oftentimes, the people who are the most pushy, loud, rude, unthinking, unconscious, or willing to fight will dominate any space they enter. A space that should be happy, quiet, creative, and inspiring, becomes dominated by whatever other person wishes to fight to gain control. Sad but true.

You know, when I first begin writing about, *"You can only play in your own playground,"* I used to see it as outside. Believing that inside would always be your own space. But, having personally dealt with personal space invasion in recent years and having seen it occur with others, I no longer limit that statement to only the outside. Sometimes, it forces its way into your inside.

Here arises the problem – *the too many rats in a cage problem*. People want their space; they want their space to be the way they want their space to be. And, it should be that way. But, it is not. There are other people in the world. And, as space becomes more and more confined as more and more people enter this world's population, those who wish to dominate (whether consciously or not) whatever space they are in, have also risen in numbers.

You can fight. I have spent the past fifty years training my body to fight. I know lawyers, philosophers, and business people who fight with their minds and they do it *very-very* well. But, for better or for worse, it is the same confrontational space. And, confrontation always equals elements of negativity.

At times, due to the actions of other people, sometimes you need to take it to the level of confrontation. Now, I can say, *"It shouldn't be that way."* And, in truth, it should not. People should never be so unconscious or aggressive that they want to dominate space where another person exists. But, the rude, the unconscious, the unthinking, the vengeful, the lustful, and the intentionally aggressive force us all into action. So, is your playground your own playground anymore? A place where you can play safely? I don't know? If you have one, I will say, *"Hold onto it dearly."* If you have a space you can exist in without the intrusion of others, love it to death because a lot of people do not have that.

So, to revise my earlier statement, *"You can only play in your own playground."* It now becomes, *"You can only play in your own playground if you have a playground to play in."*

Stealin' When I Shoulda Been Buyin'
25/March/2015 05:52 AM

A few days ago I went thought my vinyl. I know a lot of people simply collect to collect (anything) but me I prefer to collect what I actually want verse just getting stuff for stuff's sake. Anyway, it gave me the chance to move the two or three of's along, and stuff like that – keep the best of the best. It also gave me the chance to listen to some music I had not heard in a long time.

I pulled out this now deemed, *"Classic Rock,"* but back then called, *"Hard Rock,"* album I got back in high school, Uriah Heep's, *Sweet Freedom.* On this album the biggest hit was a song called, *Stealin.'* I hadn't listened to it in forever so it was fun to put it on the turntable. The chorus on the song is, *"Stealing When I Should Have Been Buying."*

I think recently we have seen a lot of this. Certainly, as I have spoken about numerous times, people do this all the time on the internet where, Stealin' is so easy. But, every now and then people go after people for their intellectual property rights stealin' and it makes the news. Marin Gaye's families big win recently over one of his songs being stolen has been all over the news. But, this is not the first time. Even George Harrison was sued and lost for his song, *"My Sweet Lord,"* as it was allegedly taken from, *"He's so fine."* Though he denied any knowable knowledge, he lost the case. Led Zeppelin has lost some big cases, as well.

When sampling began everybody grabbed everything, claiming they had the right. No, the court cases have been very clear, you can't take nothin,' not a single note. And, that is the way it should be. The big wins against Vanilla Ice and Too Live

Crew set a lot of that litigation into motion back in the 90s.

Why do you have to take somebody else's something, someone else's creation to make your own creation? Why can't your creation be whole onto itself? And, if you are going to take, at least give credit where credit is due and share in the profits.

If you give someone something, every one is happy. But, when you take something from someone, everything gets messy. I believe we can all agree when something is stolen from any of us, it makes us feel pretty crappy. Knowing that feeling, why would you do it?

And, that's the simple key to life, if something feels bad to you; it's going to feel bad to everyone. Do you want to make people feel bad? Or, do you want to be more than that?

I've dealt with this kind of stuff a bit in my own life. Those things make my attorney happy as he gets to do something. But, it should never have to be like that. Somebody's something is their something. You shouldn't take it. You shouldn't steal it. You should make your own stuff. Create your own art and let it stand on its own merits. You shouldn't be *Stealin' when you shoulda been Buyin.'*

The Law Ain't the Law or Is It?
24/March/2015 02:36 PM

I had a meeting with my attorney this morning over a distribution deal for South Asia. And, like always, whenever we get done with the business at hand we begin talking about what's going on in life. If I ever happen to be pissed off with someone or something during our meetings his eyes always get wide and he gets so excited thinking he is going to get to take legal action against someone. But, like I have said on the blog before, my lawyer always tells me I'm his worst client because I never let him sue anybody.

You know, even if I am pissed, I always try to take the high road and give people the benefit of the doubt. The fact is, being in the film game, as I am, I have been screwed over so many times it is not even funny. As an author, publishing companies have so doctored their books on me that I have never gotten paid near what I should. But really, what can you do? It happens to everyone. If you enter the game you are going to have to play by their rules. And, what does suing anybody equal? It only equals money in the attorney's bank account.

The thing is, if someone has not actually broken a specific law or violated a contract, anything you do in court has a very small chance of succeeding. It just equals time and frustration. So, why bother?

I mean, people always get upset about what other people say about them and they want to sue over that. Though I find some of the negative comments made about me pretty funny. Funny, because they are always made by someone who has not even met me or has had no interaction with me. Overall, most people like me. But, I too have had my detractors.

The fact is, the more you step into the public eye, the more haters you will develop. It doesn't matter what you do. People love to hate.

But, this is America, people can say whatever they want about you. Just look at *Yelp,* Social Media, or in many magazines and newspapers. Fact or fiction is doesn't even matter, voicing your opinion about anybody is your god given right in the United States. Maybe that's not universally right, but that is the way it is.

Me too... Sometimes people and their actions piss me off and make me angry to no end. But, even on this blog, I base my shared opinions upon provable facts and personal interaction. But, at the end of the day, I'm just like everybody else, when push comes to shove, I feel what I feel, based upon what I'm going through, and I react accordingly.

You know, it's kind of like in physical combat, the strong, the better-trained individual generally wins the fight. But, winning a fight does not necessarily equal winning the battle. For what does it really take to kick someone's ass? Just like what does it take to sue someone in a courtroom? What really matters is that we each stay as conscious of other people as possible and never try to rip them off or mess with their life. For that is the place where conflict arises. That is the place where confrontation begins. That is the place where lawyers get paid.

True life is about undoing not doing. I told that to my attorney on a follow-up call this afternoon. His response, *"You're weird."* ☺

Hit and Run
24/March/2015 07:47 AM

I always find the strange happenings of life very curious. How things and situations happen out of nowhere and they have the potential to change your life forever.

Yesterday, I was driving in *Little Saigon.* I had pulled up to a red light maybe four or five cars deep. All of a sudden I feel a strong bump. I initially thought that the car behind me must have hit me. I looked in the mirror but no. Then, I look to my side. It was a guy who smacked me with his motorcycle. He was trying to shoot in between the cars. I looked at him. He at me. Direct I contact. Young Asian male. Then bam, he bolts. Jams through traffic and he is gone. Luckily, I got his license plate number.

I pulled into a parking lot and called up the cops to file a hit and run report. They showed up a few minutes later. One in a car and one on a motorcycle. Both very nice to me. They each possessed that arrogance and internal rage ready to explode that cops always seem to harbor. They took the report. I called my insurance company and that was that.

But, that is never that. Now, I have to go and get my car appraised. I have to get the big rip in my side bumper fixed and all that. All That leading to All That unwanted life difference. But, it is the, *"All That,"* just the same. Not desired. Not asked for. But, forced to live through. And, this is the thing about life; we are each forced to live through things that we do not want to live through. Yet, people do shit to us all the time and then they bolt leaving us to deal with the consequences.

Now, hit and run happens all the time. I mean, you always hear about it on the news. Sometimes people are even killed. That is really messed up.

It has happened to me before, as well. The first time was when I was ten years old on Christmas day 1968. My father had just died and my mother had requested that my uncle drive me to her family's home in the Midwest so she could deal with the dealing. That was pretty fucked up on her part, in and of itself, but I won't go into that here. Anyway, we were driving outside of Valentine, Arizona when these two Native Americans pass us in an old truck, look at us, smile, and cut us off sending our car flying off the icy road. It was obviously intentional. Why? I will never know. But, I guess, we were pretty lucky, my uncle and I. It was a time when no one wore seat beats and though the car flipped over, we emerged relatively unscathed.

That was the first time, during that experience, that I completely released believing I was going to die. But, I didn't. Yet, there we were on the side of the highway in Arizona – we were left to deal with the aftermath of that experience. The driver of the truck, gone, gone, gone.

Another time it happened was in Hollywood in the parking lot of the supermarket on the corner of Franklin and Western in the summer of my twenty-first year. I was in the car of my then girlfriend. She was driving and from behind, bam. A junky old car runs into us hard from behind. I get out to look at the damage, the driver bolts. I jumped back in the car and we tried to follow him but he had instantly jammed at a hundred miles an hour down Western. Did he care about the damage he caused? Of course not. He just didn't want to take any responsibility for it.

This is the thing about life; people cause damage to us all the time. Do they care? Most do not. It is all like hit and run. They do it and so they don't have to deal with it, they are gone.

Like my loudmouthed neighbor who I've talked about in

some of my previous blogs. He moved in and killed the whole vib of the community with his never ending bullshit; talk, talk, talk, talk, talk. The guy has no life. All he does is stay home and talk on the phone: day and night. Does he care about the damage that he has caused my neighbors and me? No. He still talks; windows wide open. He does his damage, takes no responsibility for it, and leaves everyone else to deal with what he has created and the Life Time(s) that he has robbed. The last time I bumped into him, no, *"I'm sorry."* No nothing. In actuality, due to all the bullshit I've had to listen to from him, if I never heard his voice again that would be too soon. He never shuts up. But, just like all people who hit and run, they do what they do and don't care about what they have done to the life of others.

And, this is the thing, most people don't care about the damage they cause. They simply do not want to be held responsible for it. All they do is think about themselves. That is a bad way to live life.

You know, had the young guy riding the bike yesterday pulled over and talked to me it would have all been fine. If he didn't have insurance, which I imagine was the case, I would have just let it go and reported it to my insurance company. But, he bolted. I got his plate. Now, what will happen next, I do not know.

The thing about life is, we all do bad stuff: accidentally or not. We all have accidents. But, if we do, we need to own it. We need to fix it. And, mostly, we need to never be unconscious in our deeds and our actions and leave other people to deal with the, *"All That,"* which we have instigated.

* * *

23/March/2015 09:07 AM

Listen. Is it silent? Can you hear the silence?

If you can you are existing in the right space.

If you are the creator of noise you set the entire world into disarray.

When It Ain't the Same
23/March/2015 09:01 AM

Recently, I wrote a piece about how I believe that people should keep things changing and rearranging in their life-space, as so many people never rearrange anything and things are forever the same. All that equals is boring and the trapping of energy.

Anyway, I moved a few things around the other day. What was interesting was the reaction of my two cats.

Now, cats are very habitual creatures. They like to do what they like to do when they want to do it. They get into a pattern of time and of space and they do not want to change from that pattern. A lot of people are like this too. But, that is not good for life, for creativity, for universal energy flow or exchange, for mind space, and for the ever-new possibilities of the newness in life.

I watched as my cats keep returning to the place where they used to jump up from my couch to a bed I had for them on this unused desk. Both of them kept going there last night, looking, but not seeing. They would each spend some time sitting there curiously studying the situation, but the situation had changed. They eventually went elsewhere to develop new patterns of thought and of practice.

Have you ever watch people? ...Especially people who have a bit (or a lot) of obsessive-compulsive disorder. They want to do the same thing over and over and over again. They expect the same will be there day-after-day. But, the same is never there. Don't expect the same to be the same. Life and everything can change in a moment. Life and everything does change in a moment, It's changing right now whether you are aware of it or not. You really need to be prepared to encounter that. You really need to get out in front of that. You really need to be the sourcepoint for the change, not controlled by the change.

Change is great. It opens up all kinds of new possibilities. Don't get locked into the same. Change.

Was Your Life Better a Year Ago?
22/March/2015 08:30 AM

Was your life better a year ago? This is a question that I believe each person should ask himself or herself.

I think that we all know people; we have all met people who the first things they talk about is what they are going through and how things are bad or a least not as good as they were back then. What they are doing is comparing their life now to how their life was then. And, that's fine. Verbalizing what you feel to friends and family is all-good as long as it doesn't bring everybody down. Maybe this is you. But, though many people feel what they feel about what is going on in their life, few people ever take the time to study the reason why. Few people have the ability to truly look in the mirror and give themselves a true appraisal of what is going on in their life and why. They may justify their actions, they may blame others, they may attribute their current, less than perfect circumstances, to any number of reasons but what they rarely do is blame themselves.

All of your life is based upon what you have done. If you hurt others, you are a fault. If you damage things, you are at fault. If you lie, cheat, deceive, steal, you are at fault. Even if you believe you have a right to do the things you have done, if your life was better a year ago from where it is today, you must have done something wrong.

This is not about karma, self-guilt, or anything like that. For, the fact of the matter is, most people feel no guilt for what they have done – they could care less if they hurt or damage people or things. They feel they are entitled to do what they do when they do it and that is that. Again, few people possess the ability to take a long hard look at themselves in the mirror.

If your life is not on the path you desire; if your life is not fulfilled and abundant, if you are not living the way you want, then who else is to blame but you? You did what you did. You set a course of events into motion. Thus, you have ended up where you have ended up solely based upon what you have done.

Some people are not as selfish, unconscious, or as self-serving as the greater whole. Some people actually care enough to care. But, these people also, at times, find themselves living a life that is not ideal. But, why is this? Why is this if a person tries to give back? Commonly this occurs, in a giving person, due to the fact that they are giving from a space of ego. *"I am this." "I am giving to you." "It is I who has this to give to you." "I am doing this for you."* The central precept here is, *"I."* *"I"* is about ego. *"I"* is not about giving. The true giver has no sense of, *"I,"* in anything they do.

So, if you are at a stage of your life where you are not happy and fulfilled, if you can look back a year ago and realize life was better then, it is time to make a change. The essential thing to keep in mind is that change is not about anybody else. Change is about you. Change is not about blaming anyone or anything else. Change needs to be based upon you looking at you. Change needs to be based upon you stop doing things that hurt people or things – even if those things are justified in your own mind. Things that you may have told yourself are right but you know, deep down in inside, that you would not want them to be done to you. Mostly, change needs to be based upon you being a conduit of giving, not taking. Giving with no sense of self or ego. Giving good and positive things. Giving in silence.

Give it a try. Then, in a year, again take another look at your life. I imagine it will be better.

* * *

20/March/2015 09:47 AM

How long is your forever?

*   *   *

20/March/2015 09:47 AM

Making something worse never makes anything any better.

Some People Are Just a Problem
20/March/2015 09:40 AM

I was getting my breakfast on at *The Original Pantry* this morning – a place I recommended everyone check out at least once if you want to encounter true L.A. bohemia, especially in the deep late-night on one of those nights that you are not sleeping, for whatever reason. Anyway, this AM I walk in...

Now, *The Pantry* has this long L-shaped bar that I usually grab a stool at when I'm riding solo. As I walked in I noticed that there was this one black dude standing there taking up the space of about three stools. This, when the rest of the seats along the counter were all taken. But, the stools down at the end of the L were available so I grabbed one of those.

The waiter knows me so I got my joe and my Portuguese sausage and eggs coming my direction. I noticed that the aforementioned guy's to-go order arrived. As I sat there drinking my coffee I watched as he looked in the to-go bag and analyzed the contents of it for way too long a period of time – taking up the space of at least three customers the whole time he stood there. This, as other people who had arrived tried to find a place to sit.

My breakfast arrived. I began to eat. The guy still stood there analyzing. About half way though my meal the guy comes and plants himself right at the corner of the counter, next to where I was sitting, putting his stuff way too close to me. He began to open things up and pour salt on it and stuff like that. I sat there, almost angry, at the invasion of my space and the unconscious actions of this guy. I watched waiting for him to move his food in Styrofoam containers just one-inch closer to me at which point I would have said something that I am sure he would not have liked. But, that one-inch barrier remained.

Lucky for him. Finally, he finished doing whatever it was he was doing and left.

Me, I always wonder why people behave in this manner – obliviously to other people and what they are doing to the all and the everything around them. Why are some people so unconscious?

Some people are just a problem.

* * *

19/March/2015 09:53 AM

If you are happy about someone's injury or devastation, there is something really wrong with you.

It Was Not Easy
19/March/2015 09:46 AM

I was just discussing the old days in the martial art media industry with a person who helped me do some of the photographs for the martial art magazines I used to write for. Sadly, the publishing world has all changed and most of the magazines are gone, gone, gone. But, back then I would come up with the idea for the article, write it, and then have to get the photographs for it. Not easy...

Back then, everything was on film. So, you would do the photographs but you would never be completely sure of what you actually had until they were developed, printed, and you saw them. This was a time consuming and expensive process.

The thing was, a lot of times you, (meaning me), had to live with what you got. As you could not study the image just photographed, as you can now in the digital age, to see if it was AOK. So, you got what you got and had to live with it as reshooting was very time consuming and expensive. And, the magazines only paid me like $100.00 per article. So, a lot of the time it cost me more than that to have the photographs taken.

Most people never thought about that. I guess they still don't. They just see what they see and they never take the time to ponder what went into getting it. This is pretty much the same in all aspects of life. People just see, cast judgment based upon their limited mind frame of perception, and that is that. But, THAT is never THAT. There is always much more to THAT then can ever be known unless you know.

This process was the same with filmmaking. When we used to shoot on film, it was *very-very* time consuming and expensive. The film had to be shot. It had to be developed. It had to be transferred to be viewed, etc... Plus, you were never sure what you would come away with.

Even in the early days of filmmaking on video, of which I am told I am a pioneer, the editing was very expensive. You had to go to an editing facility, pay by the hour or the day, and once again you got what you got. All of this really taught me to work within the constraints of the, *"What you get you get,"* mindset.

Nothing in life is ever exactly the way you want it to be. This is particularly the case with artist creations. But, if you hope to DO you must learn to live within those constrains and create however you create. It may not end up perfect, it may not end up exactly the way you wanted it to be, but if you don't DO, if you don't ACCEPT what you've DONE, you own expectations will keep you from ever creating.

* * *

19/March/2015 08:33 AM

People only care when it serves their purpose.

Jai Hare Krishna
18/March/2015 01:43 PM

I was up in Koreatown today teaching a class at a friend of mine's studio. On my way home, on the corner of Pico and Western, I saw something that I had completely forgotten had ever existed; Hare Krishnas dancing and singing, *"Hare Krishna, Hare Krishna, Hare Rama, Hare Rama."*

Now, for those of us from large urban centers, who lived through the 60s, the 70s, and even into the 80s, it was not an unusual sign to see Hare Krishnas dancing, singing, and begging for money. For example, they would be in Hollywood and Westwood at night, Venice during the day, and wherever or whenever there was some sort of some sort of something going on.

The guys had shaved heads except for the small ponytail rising from the top of their head so Krishna could pull them up to heaven when they died. They wore white or orange India style clothing. The girls had long hair and wore India influenced clothing, as well. It was a total display of, *"Let's play dress up."*

They had a big center in Culver City were every Sunday night they would give anyone who arrived a big dinner and try to get them to covert. I went there once, when I was like fifteen, but it was not my scene.

To describe the four Hare Krishnas of today... There were two males and two females; all older. One of the guys looked like an aging boxer who had many been hit one too many times: grey hair and a hard face with a nose that had been broken. The lady by him wore India style clothing and was maybe in her late fifties or early sixties. She looked very wrong and out of place doing what she was doing. The other two were of the same age range but nondescript.

The thing was, where they were dancing and singing is a blighted part of L.A. I mean, it is not like they were going to covert anyone or make any bank standing there in that neighborhood.

Seeing them made me remember back to the 80s on one of my trips to India. I was waiting for my plane to board and this semi-attractive Hare Krishna girl comes up to me and tries to sell me one of their books. They used to always put pretty girls in the airports. This, of course, was before 911 when all of that kind of stuff was stopped.

Now, Prabhupada Bhaktivedanta, the founder of the Hare Krishnas, rocked in the West but though they built some temples in India, probably financed by western money, they were never highly regarded in India. I asked the girl had she ever been to India and did she understand how the Hare Krishnas were thought of there in religious circles? ...There, the sourcepoint of their religion. She ended up telling me I was fool and stormed off. Rock on little Hare Krishna girl, rock on! I wonder where she is now?

But, like I said, I had totally forgotten about them doing what they did. And, they did it everywhere! It was one of those memories simply lost from the mind. Replaced by something more important, I guess.

But, it was fun to remember a time gone past, to think back and be reminded about what was going on then. ...Then, a time when we, (myself included), believed the world was getting better by our spirituality and our good deeds and that enlightenment would reign supreme. I guess we were all taught a valuable lesson... ☺

* * *

16/March/2015 03:57 PM

What contribution to the world have you made that didn't include YOU in the equation?

* * *

16/March/2015 03:46 PM

The older you get the more things become defined by comparison: how this is compared to how that was.

Never Their Fault
16/March/2015 10:49 AM

In this world, where we have become very self-exposing, where many of us write our thoughts, feelings, and experiences via tweets, blogs, and the like, I always find it interesting how some people, when they are telling their story, almost universally make the claim(s) that it was never their fault when they do something wrong or perhaps injure the life of another through their words or actions. Sometimes you have to read between the lines to actually get it, but all things are all things and what they write is presented from a very self-serving point of view.

You know, the thing is, a lot of people don't write. They are busy living their life, doing their job, making their money, paying their bills, and raising their family. From this, they are the one's who are truly giving to society. Then, there are others, some who make their living via the various methods on the internet; they are the one's who have the time to write. And, if they possess the predilection for writing, they are the ones who present their thoughts to the world and/or their interpretations of reality.

Here's the thing, *your reality is your reality.* That is your business. What you think is what you think. That is also your business. But, the moment you bring anyone or anything else into your discussion, that becomes the business of the person about whom you speak, as well. And, here is where karma is born. Here is where the reason for making excuses is founded. Because what you have said or what you have done has affected someone else. If what you have said or have done has hurt the life of anyone, in anyway, then you are responsible for that damage. And, here is the sourcepoint for the writing of what I was just speaking of – for the claiming of why you did what your did and why you said what you said. But, at the end of the day, all that writing, all that justifying means is nothing, if you have hurt someone else. Though you may write very well-versed explanations, based upon your own perception of reality, that does not change the action(s) that you set in motion.

I often wonder, what will/would happen to these people if they had to make a living the old way, the real way, and could not find a way to create income via grabbing and poking at the creations or the lives of others on the internet. Certainly, in this age of internet/Reality TV stardom there is a different set of factors at play. But, do you ever consciously question what that means to the overall whole and/or the greater good. It is kind of like if you ever go to one of those comic con, horror, or sci-fi type of gatherings – If a girl is dressed in a costume; no matter how pretty she is or is not, the boys and the men, without a sense of self-purpose, will flock to her, wanting to take photographs and all that. But, what does that equal and why is that a life-factor? The answer is, people want the THAT. The THAT which they can't have but dream about having. That same girl, in the world of reality, may not even be considered that attractive, but place her in the right situation or on the right stage and she is a star. That is great for her. But, all that does is lead to the ongoing desire for THAT. THAT which one cannot have. And, here lies the secret to success via the world of the internet, (for both women and men), create an image that someone wants but cannot have and then put it out there. From this, a person is given an internet voice. But, what does that voice actually equal when it takes from others, hurts others, and then makes excuses and justifications for these actions?

You know, as someone who has been on the internet since before it was even called the internet, I have witnessed a lot about this world of cyberspace. But, mostly what I have seen is the robbing, the taking, the hurting, and the not caring about the repercussions. People take because they can take. People steal because they can steal. People hurt others because they can hurt others with little or no consequence. Then, some people actually write well-worded definitions for doing what they do. From this, they rally those who are in their camp to see their point of view. Right or wrong, that is the way it is. But, that should not be the way it is.

As someone who has created certain things, I often see people making money from of my creations on the internet. Whether that is charging a membership fee to see movies that I have created and they have upload and offer for, *"Free Download,"* or whether it was a website someone recently pointed me to where the *Site Lord* took historic research that took me years upon years to compile and they took it, reworded it a bit here and there, and called it their own without even referencing me as the source. As wrong as I see all this, as I am the creator of the said products, people don't care. They take because they can take and they damage because they can damage.

Now, I can say, *"That is wrong,"* until I am blue in the face. I can proclaim to the people that take and then make excuses for their taking, (to themselves and to all those who will read their excuses), *"What you're doing is simply not right."* But, it does not matter what I say. The only think that matters is if you possess a strong enough moral compass to simply not do or say bad things. Few people have this, however. They want to make their bank and they do not care who pays the price for the price. Some may say, *"This is the way it has always been."* And, they are right. Throughout history people have taken without caring, people have hurt others without caring, and they have done it so they could get by, get over, and be seen as something more. ...That was and is the way it is, but is that right? No, it is not. But, the moral compass has to begin with you. And, here's the key, if you must justify or explain your actions that have hurt, taken from, or damaged someone's life, instead of writing well-verse explanations, you should be writing an apology and then go about righting your wrongs.

If you are taking from others, that action in itself let's you know you are wrong. If your words or actions hurt others, that let's you know you are wrong. If you are justifying your actions to yourself or to others, that let's you know you are in the wrong.

Be more. Don't take. Give. Provide true, organic, self-created thoughts, things, and words to the world. Then, you don't have to make excuses.

You Should Never Have To Feel Anger
16/March/2015 08:51 AM

Why do you become angry with a person? The reason you become angry is that they have done something that has damaged your life.

We all want what we want out of life. The problem arises, however, in that what you want may not be what I want, just as what I want may not be what you want.

In life, few people care enough about the other person to put their own desires aside and not force another person to be dominated by what they want or what they have done. From this, all kinds of chaos is given birth to. This is the cause for all level of interpersonal violence, deception, retribution, and, of course anger.

You did something that hurt another person, thus, they are angry with you. You did something without thinking about another person, thus, your actions drove another person to anger.

Anger does not exist in a person who has not been harmed by someone else. Anger is based in what someone else has done.

You have no right to judge or take from someone to give to yourself. You have no right to believe that you know more than anyone else or you have something to say or do if what you say or do damages the life of anyone.

You cannot believe that you know what is right or better for a person or persons. That is simply ego. You are not all-knowing. No one is.

If a person becomes angry with you that means you did something that damaged their life. The fault, therefore, is solely with you.

Do you cause other people to become angry? How many people are angry with you? The reason for their anger is you and what you have done. What does that say about the choices you have made? Were your choices made with the betterment of the other person on your mind or where they only made by you hoping to gain what you hoped to gain? If someone is angry with you, the answer to that question is obvious.

If someone, anyone is angry with you, you are the one at fault.

Old School Verses New School
14/March/2015 08:33 AM

I have this one friend who has just been accepted into a university to go for a graduate degree that will help them in their field of employment. More and more it has become required that you possess very specific graduate degrees if you hope to maintain your position and/or climb the corporate ladder.

The funny thing in this process is that they are going to school via an online process. This is obviously the new trend in education; particularly for advanced education. I asked them what was the process: what were they going to do, how were the classes structured, and stuff like that? They had no idea. They are simply supposed to sign in when the class begins and all will be revealed.

We both laughed about this. They said, *"Isn't that they way school always was? You didn't really know what was going on until you went to class."* I jokingly replied, *"No, you knew that you were going to have to buy a very expensive textbook that you were not going to even need, you were going to have to show up between nine and ten on Monday, Wednesday, and Friday, and you were going to be bored to tears."* We both laughed.

Education is changing. Great/thoughtful companies like Starbucks are even paying so their employees can get their college degrees online. Me, I am frequently asked to teach university level courses online. I always turn those offers down. It is not that I am too Old School it is just that I am not that New School. I believe education needs to be face-to-face for the experience to be whole and real.

Welcome to the new age where there is no personal

interaction only a computer screen sitting in front of your face.

Sounds like a Sci-Fi movie from the '50s. ☺

Shake It Up
13/March/2015 02:32 PM

How often do you change the environment of where you live? Meaning, do you ever rearrange things or are they the same way they have been forever?

I know some people that as long as I have known them; nothing has changed in their living space: their couch, their table, their bed, their desk, their everything is locked into position, never to be moved again.

I don't know, that just seems so strange to me. ...To be so locked into a specific framework for your environment that you never even consider replacing your placement.

Me, I always move things around. Then, it will stay that way for a day, a week, a year, but then it is removed; keeping things fresh, new, allowing for new reactions and experiences.

People, also, always seem to have a very specific way in which they believe their furniture should be arranged. The bed must be up against a wall. The chest of drawers must be up against a wall. The desk should be over there. The bookshelf that way.

Every now and then I go into someone's place and their arrangement is a complete mishmash of they way things, *"Should,"* be. Totally different. Totally wrong. Man, that is so refreshing. It is so inspirational.

What am I saying? I am saying, *"Shake it up."* Move your stuff around. Get free. Be free. Do something different. It will open up a whole new world of possibilities and experiences for you.

God is Looking Out for Me
13/March/2015 02:31 PM

I popped into check out one of my local thrift stores today. Working, was this guy I have come to know over the past several years. Whenever I see him we make small talk. This guy is the exact same age as me and he grew up in the Los Angeles area. Though we live very different lives, due to our age and where we grew up, we possess a very similar mindset of timeframe experiences.

When I have spoken to him over the past few months he was having problems with his roommate. The guy was in recovery but fell back into using crack. As such, he didn't pay the rent and they were getting evicted from their apartment.

The roommate is out on the street. The thrift store guy found a Sober House where he could live.

A Sober House is a living environment set up my various organizations where the people are all in recovery and must stay that way to live there. Though they pay rent, their actions are very monitored.

The guy was telling me about his living environment. He has four male roommates in his bedroom and several others in the various other bedrooms around the house.

I, of course, was very positive; telling him now he didn't have to worry about getting evicted and he didn't have to deal with the various other problems his roommate had been causing him. He looked at me, smiled, and said, *"God is looking out for me."*

I'm glad he thinks that way but what he said sent me to thinking. If I believed that living in a Sober House with a shit load of other male roommates was god looking out for me, I would fucking kill myself. I would put a bullet right in my brain. Now, to me, god looking out for me would be him (or her) hooking me up with a multi-million dollar house on the beach. But, that isn't happening, so I guess he doesn't care. I guess I'm screwed. ☺

This is the thing about life; we each perceive reality the way we perceive reality. We each see blessings and curses defined by our own set of definitions. To him, moving into a Sober House made all things AOK. And, that's great! I'm so happy for him. But, his reality is not my reality.

The fact of life is, the simpler you live, the simpler you can be, the more accepting you can be of the small gifts of life, the easier your life becomes.

The Demon Seed
13/March/2015 09:13 AM

In each of us there is an element, a behavior that works against the greater good. No one of us is absolutely pure and without sin; no one of us has not done something that has hurt someone else.

In life, through human interaction, moral schooling, and personal development we each come to understand what is the right way to behave and which is the wrong way to behave. From this, we come to understand the things that we should not do and keep those less than ideal elements of our personal self in check. This generally occurs, at the latest, by our late adolescence or early adulthood. From this, we travel through life causing as little damage as possible.

Some people, however, due to chosen influences or physiological or psychological damage continue on a pathway of embracing their own inner darkness and spewing it out to the world. From this, they continue on a pathway of hurting the life or lives or others and doing things that are against the greater good. Though these people may feel momentary empowerment or emotional release by preforming these actions, they are the ones who end up alone, friendless, isolated, and even end up in places like mental institutions and prisons.

Every time you do something that hurts someone, every time you consciously destroy or break something, every time you knowingly take from someone or something, every time you lie, every time you allow your emotional self to overrule your conscious self and take control over your actions, you are performing a bad act. You know this. Yet, some people decide to not exercise control over these elements of their life. Why? Commonly, it is because they have been allowed to get away with it for a long period of time and the act of the actions has not forcibly been held in check. Or, it is due to the fact that they surround themselves with people or a thought process that condones acts that damage the lives of others.

Whether you have been disciplined as a child, as an adult, or never at all, you know what is right and what is wrong; you know the right way to behave. You know that by acting in a particular manner your actions have the potential to hurt and damage the lives of others. Just like in the movies where the religious figure calls out to a demon inhabiting the body of a person, *"In the name of our lord, be gone!"* You too must be forceful with yourself if you find that you cannot simply exist in a life-space of consciousness and working towards the greater good for all.

Take and maintain control of the demon seed in you. The longer you are good, the less control negativity will hold over you.

* * *

12/March/2015 04:25 PM

What you can do you can do but what you can't do you can't do. Stop lying to yourself.

* * *

12/March/2015 04:21 PM

    You have to know where you're going if you ever hope to get there.

* * *

12/March/2015 10:06 AM

Everybody has an excuse.

Human Behavior
12/March/2015 09:56 AM

The very first psychology course I ever took, when I was a young college student, was a class called, Human Behavior. I actually took it as one of my general ed. requirements. Prior to that I was trying to discover what I really wanted to study in college. First, I was a Philosophy major, but there was way too much statistical mathematics that goes hand-in-hand with that subject. For those of you who may not know, on the university level, philosophy is a lot about statistics and calculations, not simply about thought. I was never very good at math so that major went by the wayside. My next major was Religious Studies but that department was way too western orientated for my tastes.

Anyway... The class was great. It was taught by this, on the younger side of middle age, Ph.D., who was very open and into all of the new thought that was prominent in the 1970s. He would sometimes ask for a hug at the end of class and I would inevitably be the only one who would ever go up and give him one – the rest of the students being way too uptight. ☺

But there, in that class, I found an applicable way to integrate a lot of the understandings I was developing about humanity into a cohesive thought process. It opened the doorway for me to actually come to study, with a concise framework, human behavior. Which is something I have always done and have continued to do.

Ever since I was young boy I have enjoyed reading autobiographies and books and articles written about specific people. From those, you can truly peer into the human mind and a person's motivations for doing what they do. Certainly, each are written from a specific point of view detailing to the reader only a specific aspect of human behavior that the author wants you to know. But, *none-the-less,* that too reveals a lot about human behavior – the human behavior of the author.

If you wish to truly study and learn from human behavior the first thing to do is to turn off your preconceived notions, ideologies, and judgments when you meet a person and simply let them be them. But, instead of simply living your moment with them, watch, study, and analyze what they are saying and what they are doing. From this, through time and analysis, you will come to understand why a person is doing what they are doing and how their behavior affects your life and the greater life-space on the whole.

In life, it seems that there is a very common propensity for people to want to talk about someone else, discuss what they think about them and put their own definitions upon that person. They do this from a very limited perspective in that they are only viewing the external – placing their own personal judgment(s) upon that person, and then stating it to the world. If you wish to study human behavior this is an ideal example of a person who possess the *holier-than-thou* mindset. They believe that they are so all-knowing that they have the right to pass judgment on others. Though this is a very common mindset, it is not a healthy one to associate with. The reason being, this type of person passes judgment on everyone. They most commonly do this in order to shift the focus from themselves, as they do not want people to look too deeply into who and/or what they truly are. If they can keep the focus elsewhere, their true self will not be discovered by the outside world.

On the other side of the issue, there is the person who is very self-inspective. This person prefers to study themselves before they look to others. They focus on initially making themselves better, instead of passing judgment upon others.

Through time and life, the person who cares enough to truly care decides the best way to pass through life in the most giving, caring, and non-judgmental way possible. The thing is, via the study of human behavior, we can each come to understand who is actually a caring and giving person and who is a person that is simply projecting that mindset to draw people to them to feed their ego.

Here is the thing you really need to look for if you hope to actually give-back to life and to help humanity without falling prey to possessing a misplaced sense of self-worth. First of all, shun the ego driven people from your life. They are not the true teacher, nor are they a good person. Do not let them be your guide for they will send you down the wrong path.

Here, in life, we are all humans. We interact with humans on a daily basis. Each of us possesses a defined sense of Self. But, how many of us actually personally define that sense of Self as opposed to simply letting our wants, desires, and our inner demons control that Self?

First, look to your personal human behavior and come to find out whom you truly are. Do this first, before you do anything else. From there, you must decide what you want to do with who you are and what you have to offer.

Now, here is the tricky part. You may find that want to be something big or great. You may have the desire to be seen as something grand. But, if you possess that desire, that desire in itself, tells you that you are walking down the wrong road. That is a road of desire that is not the pathway of giving, caring, and helping.

The person who gives and never takes is the true saint. They are the ones who deserve admiration not the person who tells you what they think about you or about other people.

Life is simple. What do you want to be? If you don't know why you want to be it, you don't know.

Life is simple. Why do you do the things you do? If you don't know why you do the things you do or if the things you do are out of control and your emotions control you, than what does that say about you?

Study human behavior. Study your own human behavior. Study other people's human behavior. From this, define what is right, giving, and caring. Become more. Become someone who gives and doesn't take.

Whine, Whine, Whine, Bitch, Bitch, Bitch
11/March/2015 03:59 PM

I don't believe that there is anyone who is one-hundred percent perfectly happy with their all and their everything. Yes, yes, from a metaphysical perspective we can say, *"All is perfect,"* and allow ourselves to fall into that mindset. And, some people do this very well. Good for them! But, on a more reality-based note, I don't think anyone would not like something to be at least a little bit different in his or her life. Maybe this was something to have happened differently in the past. Maybe it is for something to be better or more complete in the here and the now. Or, maybe it is some dream that will happen in the future. This is everybody... Everybody wants life and life things to be better.

In life, there are three primary breeds when it comes to making things better. One, there is the person who constantly tries and strives to make their life and the lives of others better and more whole. Two, there is the person who dreams for it to be so but takes no action (for whatever reason). Three, there is the person who does nothing but complain about their life, their past, their present, and their unfulfilled dreams for the future; whine, whine, whine, and bitch, bitch, bitch is all that they do. They complain to everyone who will lend them an ear.

Why a person behaves in any of the three mindsets can, of course, go back to all kinds of personal psychological determinants. But, whatever the cause or the case, a person emerges into one of these three categories. Who are you?

I think, from an analytical perspective, we all will say that the person who constantly tries is the most aped to achieve what they truly want out of life. The person who doesn't try is stuck. And, the person who is a consummate whiner is the one who brings everyone down. Okay... But, then what?

This is the thing... Are you oblivious to what people think and say about you when you are not around them? Because if all you are is a whiner and a complainer, how do you think people truly feel about you? If all you do is to discuss all you are not and what you don't have, first of all you are very selfish, secondarily all you do is bring everyone else down. How does that help you achieve your dreams and how does that make other person feel about you?

The truth of life is we are one hundred percent responsible for where we find ourselves. What we did in the past, lead us to where we are now. If we have hurt people, if we have damaged their lives, if we are not currently living the repercussions, we soon will be. Just as if we have selflessly helped other people, (asking for nothing in return), if we are not yet receiving the benefits, we soon will be.

The problem with people who are trapped in their own sense of lack of life fulfillment and thereby are doing nothing but complaining about it is, they are not truly taking a long hard look at themselves. What they are doing is simply projecting their dissatisfaction onto others, thereby bringing other people down. All this does is set a course of events into motion where nothing ever gets any better.

We all want a better life. But, if we do not turn off our own desires and turn our attentions towards the betterment of others, then all we will be is lost in what we are not and/or do not have.

Be more than someone who just thinks about himself or herself. Be someone who thinks and cares about others first and foremost. From this, your life will instantly get better.

Dysfunctionally Insane
11/March/2015 01:53 PM

I was cruising down the thoroughfare today and decided to stop in at a *Goodwill* to see if they had any interesting vinyl. As I walked passed the dishes and glassware section I noticed this guy precisely stacking various bowls, dishes, cups, and glasses on a table. He was doing it like he was one of those balancing experts. I noticed he didn't like one cup, so he reached around himself, studied his options, and grabbed another one. He then set it upon a plate that was stacked atop a bowl that had a glass in it.

This guy was just an average looking white guy, wearing a tee shirt and shorts. But, there he was, doing what he was doing as if it truly meant something.

I went and checked out their albums and CDs. Nothing of interest so I was moving towards the door. There he still was, arranging the dishes and the glassware.

Now, it is not like he created some great structure with his endeavor. There was just something very obsessionally broken in this guy's mind making him think that there was some order to the universe that only he understood and could orchestrate.

One can only question what was going on in his brain. It is one of those things that if you didn't see it, you would never even think about it or even believe that someone would do something like that – go to a *Goodwill* to stack bowls, plates, and dishes. Strange...

A bit later in the day, I was in another parking lot walking towards my car. Out of nowhere this guy screams, *"Fuuucccckkkk,"* at the top of his lungs. I mean, he was really loud. Everyone around me, including myself, was a bit shocked and looked to see what was going on. But, nothing was.

Again, just an average looking white guy. But, something, somewhere, lost to only his mind, he decided he needed to vent. We can only wonder why.

Life is a strange place. Most people are pretty functional, even if they are a little on their weird side. But, there they were, two examples of the dysfuncationally insane. Normal looking. But, no where near normal.

* * *

11/March/2015 08:57 AM

Take an educated guess. How much longer do you have to live?

At the end of today you will have one less day of life.

How do you want to live today?

* * *

10/March/2015 01:59 PM

You should only forgive the people who deserve forgiveness.

Don't Behave Like a Fourteen Year Old Teenage Girl
10/March/2015 01:58 PM

Have you ever encountered an adult male who talks and talks on the telephone? They tell anyone who will listen to them what they think about this subject or that person. They gossip, they try to make themselves sound like some sort of expect, they make up lies about themselves and embellish any small life experience they may have had. I imagine that this is all based upon self-deception or personal insecurity for never having actually accomplished anything of value with their life, for if they had, they would be doing that instead of simply talking.

On the TV series, the sitcoms, and in the movies, the young teenage girl is always portrayed as the one who talks and talks, gossips and gossips, on the telephone. For them, at that age, that is fine. That is what they are doing. But, for an adult, who behaves in this adolescent manner, all they are doing is wasting their lifetime, the life of those who may listen to them, and damning the lives of those around them who are forced to listen to their conversations.

The doers do. The talkers talk but do nothing.

From a personal perspective, even when I was young, my friends and I would get on the phone, say what needed to be said, and save any other conversation for personal contact. Because personal contact is the only true contact. We never wasted our lives or the lives of others by talking and saying nothing.

There is this amusing series of commercial for DIRECTV in rotation right now where the actor Rob Lowe portrays himself as the handsome, successful Rob Lowe and then he plays himself as some sort of a loser Rob Lowe. One of them has DIRECTV, the other has cable. At the end of each commercial he says, *"Don't be like this me..."* And, that is just it, either be good, helpful, and successful, or shut the fuck up!

Don't behave like a fourteen-year-old teenage girl.

* * *

10/March/2015 09:50 AM

What you did you did and the repercussions never go away.

I Don't Care About You
10/March/2015 09:40 AM

"I don't care about you. I only care about what you've done to my life."

Most people do not care about any one or any thing that they are not personally involved with. The only way that you even know about another person is if they enter your life in one way or the other.

If you don't know about them, you don't care about them. This is the simple fact of humanity. And, I use the term, *"Humanity,"* in the broadest sense of the word.

When we think of personal interaction and person-to-person involvement the first thought that comes to mind is generally via the means of letting a person into our life. For example, you meet them, you like them or you dislike like them, you define your relationship, and that is that. But, this is not always the case. Many people force their way into our lives; people that we would never have even known existed if they did not target us. This can come via so many means: stalking, internet attacks, forced interpersonal meetings that they have orchestrated but pretend are random, and the list goes on. But, once this person is in your life, once you know about them, you are then forced to deal with the repercussions of their actions in association with your life.

Some people enter our lives and everything becomes better but then there is the case of just the opposite. Some people enter our lives and truly destroy many facets of our existence. The thing is, if a person enters our realm via normal means, and if they damage us, we can generally get them out of our lives via normal methods. But, this is not always the case;

especially if they come at us out of left field – come at us via some way where there is no definable method to make them leave.

This is where life and interpersonal relationship get complicated. And, this is where you need to take a look at yourself, how and why you interact with other people, and what effect are you having upon those people.

Like I have long spoken about, people feel an abstract and misdirected sense of empowerment any time they dish out a judgment about another person or when they or their friends are discussing someone in a negative manner. *"Yeah, this person is that!"* But, this is not how true personal empowerment should be given birth to. For the moment anything is born through negativity, all that it can breed is further negativity; which always comes back to hurt the person who has initiated it in the first place.

The reason I speak about this is due to the fact that this is the reason many people enter the life or another person. They come via the guise of negative assessment of someone else's life. If you do this, all that occurs is distaste on the part of the person's life you have entered and from this all that is born is future/further negativity that will come back to define your existence.

How do you meet people? How do other people find out about you? How do you enter the life of another people? And, once you have entered their life, how do you affect their life?

These are important questions you need to ask yourself. What are you creating in life?

Mad At You
10/March/2015 09:40 AM

There is an interesting phenomenon that takes place in life that occurs when you are mad at someone but they are the one who is right or, perhaps better stated, you are mad at someone but you are the one who is in the wrong.

Life is a selfish place. People think about themselves first and rarely ever take others into consideration before doing what they do. From this, all kinds of anger is given birth.

But doing, whatever a person does, and whether or not you consider that action right or wrong, is solely based upon a personal point of view. This is the same with anger. Anger, directed towards someone, is only based upon your own individual point of view.

If what a person does makes you happy or does something for the betterment of you, then all is well with the world. But, if they do something that you don't like, something that is for the betterment of them and doesn't benefit you, your anger arises and who knows what actions that will lead you to.

Few people care enough to care about another person first. Most people prefer to React rather than to Act in a conscious, considerate manner. If your anger is based upon your own set of desires being shunned, then that makes you a very selfish person.

Think about it, how many times has someone become angry with you? Was their anger based upon something that you did bad or wrong to them? If it was, then their anger was justified. But, if their anger was based upon some nondescript action you took, that had no direct affect on them, then what was the reason for them to become angry?

This is the same with you. Think about the last time you were angry with someone. Was it because of them doing something bad to you or was it simply because of them defending their rights or being true to themselves? If you become angry with someone else because they are defending themselves due to something you personally said or something you set into motion and was damaging that other person in some manner, then that is truly a case of you possessing misplaced anger.

Anger is a choice. Why you become angry is also a choice. If you can make yourself rise above selfish, self-based anger, think how much freer you will be and how much more peaceful the entire world will become.

Would You Work for Free?
08/March/2015 08:35 AM

A friend of mine asked me to come and speak to a university class he teaches on filmmaking last week. When we got to the Q&A segment of the talk the subject of internet piracy of films came up as it often does. I asked the students, *"How many of you have a job?"* Some of the students raised their hands. I then questioned, *"Of those of you who have a job, how many of you would work if you didn't get paid? How many of you would work for free?"* Of course, nobody raised their hands.

The subject then shifted to some claiming that they are poor college students and they can't afford to pay to see movies and various comments like that. But, that does not change the primary premise, if you wouldn't do something for free, why do you think it is right to steal from someone else's income?

People rarely live their life based upon morality. Most, live what they live, take whatever it is they can get away with, and do not even give a thought to any one or any thing. Few people ever think about the implications of their actions and how those actions affect other people.

Now, I could talk forever attempting to get people to care about the greater good and what it right and what is wrong, but who would listen? If you don't care, you don't care. And, people never care until something affects them personally. Right or wrong that is the way it is. But, the truth is, it does not have to be that way. If you care about humanity, if you care about your rights and the rights of other people, particularly those who create something, then doing the right thing can and should begin with you.

Don't do it! Don't steal. Don't take away the income of other people. Don't steal people's artistic creations so you can save a buck or make a buck. Let doing the right thing begin with you.

* * *

07/March/2015 08:03 AM

Everything you are is either everything you accepted or everything you created.

Days of Technology
07/March/2015 08:01 AM

There was never a moment in my life that I was not exposed to TV. In fact, my entire life has been defined by watching it. There were some shows that I loved as a kid. And, this has progressed throughout my life. There are some shows that I love today.

On the spiritual circuit, TV has always been looked down upon. It is this and it is that but the one thing that it is not is spiritual. But, look to great TV shows like the original *Kung Fu* TV series. Great spirituality! A person could learn all they need to know about how to live a spiritual life by watching that series.

On the other side of the issue is the fact that many spiritual teachers, from the time it was available foreword, have used TV technology to get their message out there. I have been a part of that.

I was Swami Satchidananda's soundman for a number of years. I would go up and down the west coast and record every lecture and/or talk he gave. I took my PA system, my microphones, my mixer, my 4-track reel-to-reel and my cassette deck with me and recorded everything. I wish you would have known me then. ☺

Though time and technology has moved on and most of that equipment is long gone, I still have one of the mics that Gurudev used to speak into. I guess some would consider that pretty holy.

Anyway, how many of those recordings have survived I do not know as I always gave my tapes over to the powers that be. But, what I do know is that I recorded it.

Hand-in-Hand with my recording his lectures, there was this one guy, Kumar, who videotaped his lectures. It was done via an early system of relatively portable video, where video was recorded via a camera onto a one-inch tape. Again, I do not know how much of that video footage has survived. But, it was video taped and I was there helping the guy set his system up.

And, here is the thing, in spiritual circles TV is bad, technology is bad, but it was, none-the-less, used to record an era for future generation to learn from.

For how do we learn? We learn by listening to our teachers.

The funny thing was, none of Satchidananda's ashrams: *Yogaville East* and *West* had a TV, nor did the various Integral Yoga Institutes around the country. They were, *"Froboden."* I'm jokingly using the German term as it sounds so much more imposing. Yet, there we were, casting Gurudev's words to eternity with his approval.

Life and technology has continued to expand. I am what I am because of the influence they have had upon me. Whether it was watching cartoons as a kid, watching Richard Hittleman teaching yoga on an L.A. UHF station when I was eight, or recording the lectures of a great conduit of Eastern Spirituality as I transitioned from my teen years to adulthood, it has defined my life. Just as it has defined the lives of all of those of my generation and the next and the next.

Is technology spiritual? Yes, it is. For it gives us the keys to the past and the future. It provides us with a method of easily accessible True Learning.

Exposing Your Wounds
06/March/2015 10:22 AM

I believe that everyone in life has experienced moments that empowered them and moments that truly hurt, leaving a scar – sometimes a scar for life. Some people's lives are lucky and they have experienced very few negative life elements or they have the psychological makeup to simply blow them off. Others are not so blessed, however, and they become defined by their wounds. Of course, there are those who fall somewhere in between.

Though there are some people who are very outspoken about their wounds, feeling that it is important to tell everyone the truth about what defines them as a person, most people are not like that. They hide their wounds and keep them from the world. They only expose them to those who become very close to them or in some cases they keep them hidden and locked into their own mind forever.

There has long been a lot of psychologically based talk about the need to open up and let the dark moments of your life been seen. It is stated that from this you will gain mental release and psychological freedom. But, is that true? Have you ever told someone something in confidence, something very personal – told it to someone that you thought was your friend and then they used it against you or they broadcast it to anyone who would listen. Did that action free you in any way? Probably not.

People define other people by their own internal system of judgment. They hear what a person has to say and then they pass judgment on those words or that person's life experience. If a person is conscious, they listen, they hear, and they attempt to understand. If a person is self-involved, unconscious, or self-loathing, they take all they hear, reevaluate it in their own mind; place their own misguided since of definitions upon it, and use it to their own ends. As wrong as this is, this is the way many people behave.

In each of us, there is that place where we hurt. In some cases, in some people, that hurt defines their entire existence. It keeps them from moving forward and becoming all that they could have been. It may cause them to be mean, evil-spirited, and cruel to other. In fact, some people take their own life due to the life definition of hurt.

But, where does that hurt come from? Hurt comes to us by the actions of others. Or, it comes to us by the words of others who define our existence by their own limited frame of mind. Therefore, all of life is defined by the words, deeds, and actions of other people. As wrong as that may be, that is the truth. To this end, each of us, who desires to live a life based upon consciousness, must be acutely aware of what we are saying and what we are doing to others.

Yes, others are your responsibility! In fact, the whole world is your responsibility, because everything you say and everything you do sets an entire course of events into motions. If your words and deeds are good and positive, they are good and positive and they evoke positive life events. If they are not, they are not and people can become hurt by them.

And, if you don't care about hurting others, what does that say about you? If you don't care about hurting others, what makes you think that you should not be hurt?

Many people make a big mistake in life when what they say or what they do provides them with a sense of empowerment. But, if what they are saying and what they are doing is based upon a negative ideology or if what they are saying or what they are doing is hurting the life of another person, only negative life events will be set in motion by those actions. From this, hurt is given birth to.

Before you say or do anything, look deeply into your self and study your own life hurt. Then, move forward and only do and say things that will cause no more of that life hurt to any one or any thing.

* * *

06/March/2015 08:55 AM

If your deeds and actions hurt others, why do you believe you should not be hurt?

* * *

06/March/2015 08:54 AM

If you base your life upon a lie, all you will encounter is liars.

* * *

06/March/2015 08:53 AM

What happens when you ask god for help and no help arrives?

* * *

06/March/2015 08:53 AM

    Do you think that a sane person believes that they can speak with angels or demons?

* * *
06/March/2015 08:32 AM

Do you think that any sane person would believe that they are so special that they can personally harness the power of god?

The Amazing Randi
04/March/2015 02:07 PM

As I was driving this afternoon I was listening to Madeline Brand's show on KCRW, *Press Play.* She did a great interview with The Amazing Randi.

The Amazing Randi is a guy who came to prominence, at least in my mind, when he made frequent appearances on The Johnny Carson Show back in the '70s debunking people who claimed they had supernatural powers like Uri Geller. Throughout my teenage years I watched *The Johnny Carson Show* every night and I totally remember each of his appearances.

Aside from Uri Geller, he also debunked the claims of people like Satya Sai Baba by replicating the ash falling from a jug, as Sai Baba claimed he was able to produce the ashes from the gods. And, he also replicated the techniques of so-called spiritual healers in the Philippines who, at the time, claimed they had the power to enter a person's body with their hands, removes the cancer or whatever else ailed them, and then seal them up again as if nothing had happened.

It was a great interview, as I did not even know The Amazing Randi was still alive. And, he once again, as he did back then, called out and chastised the claims and actions of what he (and I) define as, *"Frauds."* And, that is exactly what they are, people who take advantage of the need in some people to tap into a greater power and then charge them money. As he stated, *"Some of these people have gotten very rich over what they claim."* That is so wrong!

As I've discussed in this blog (The Scott Shaw Zen Blog 5.0) and in my previous blogs, in recent years, I was forced to encounter a complete spiritual fraud in the case of a guy who moved in next-door to me. One minute he would be screaming, *"Fuck me! Fuck me and mine,"* over and over and over again and the next he would be charging people to give them spiritual advice. As I've said before, I don't even know how a person like that can live with themselves. They should be so ashamed of their actions. But, there he was and is.

In kind of referencing my previous blog, that *mutha fucker* robbed a good portion of my life and the other neighbors who live around him by his loud, unthinking, bullshit behavior. And, he fucking owes me! Thankfully, he has become a little quieter but that does not give me back the life lost.

And, this is the thing about frauds, they make claims but they are never what they claim to be. If they were, they would not harm the life of anybody. They would only help people and, most of all, they would not charge for doing it. Did Mother Theresa charge to help the lepers? No, she did not.

In the interview, The Amazing Randi thinks very much the same way as I do in that these frauds cater to a need some people have to believe in a greater power and believe that some people can actually harness that greater supernatural, spiritual power. He referenced one lady who went to this religious healer. Randi and his team went and spoke to her before she was called to the stage. She had serious leg problems and could not walk without the help of two crutches. She explained how much she believed in this man and his powers. She went on stage, the man claimed to heal her, and broke one of her crutches. She was then led off the stage being held up by two of the healer's assistance. When The Amazing Randy encountered her later that evening she again was using two crutches but she believed it was her own fault. She believed that she wasn't faithful enough or the healing would have worked. How sad is that?

For most of us, we see the flaw in her logic. But, this is power these fraudulent people possess. It is never their fault; it is your fault for not believing hard enough or not having enough faith.

At the root of the problem, which provides these people with their power, is that many of us, in times of turmoil and uncertainty, turn to a higher power. And, this is where these frauds find their audience. They don't care about the lies they tell, some may even believe their own lies, but if they were true to themselves the first thing any of them would speak is the truth about who and what they truly are and not pretend to be some holier than thou healer, medium, psychic, guru, or whatever. And, this is the thing about frauds, all they do is project a sense of knowledge and superiority and claim, I am something that you are not, but I can pass my knowledge or my healing onto you for a price. That is just wrong!

The main thing in all this is, be strong onto yourself. Even in times of sickness, pain, or sorrow, never fall prey to these people. Because if you saw (or in my case heard) who and what these people truly are, you would never go to them for anything.

How Do You Replace Life Lost?
04/March/2015 09:31 AM

In each of our lives there are the times where we find ourselves being very happy in doing what we do and then there are times that are defined by just the opposite. ...Those times when we are forced into situations where we feel our life is being robbed from us. These times can be motivated by many factors: bad relationships, bad neighbors, bad co-workers, or bad people infiltrating our life-space. But, the sourcepoint for all of these times is defined by one thing, the negativity of another person's actions for the silent and the caring cause no life dilemmas, whereas the unconscious, the uncaring, and the egotistical, cause many.

People are the cause and the causation for all of life's experiences. Meaning, what they do (what you do) sets all of life in motion. What you say, what you do, how you act, where you choose to place yourself, sets the next course of life events in motion. Therefore, what you do and what they do defines all of this life-space.

What do you do? How do you act? What do you say? And, how do you behave?

Is what you are doing making those around you feel better? Or, is what you are doing hurting the life of others? Look at your life and you will know the answer to that question.

If you have hurt one person you have hurt the whole world. For all of life springs forth from one singular action – add to that equitation and all of existence is defined.

The fact is, most people only think about themselves when they do whatever it is that they do. Do you? Most do not think or care about the affect they are having on others. Do You? In some cases, people actually escalate themselves into a position where they knowingly know that what they do has the potential to affect others. And, from that position they began down a pathway of conscious destruction of the lives of others. They say things, they do things, and they set events in motion where all that is left is the demise of any sense of happiness that the other person possesses. Still others are so unconscious of their actions that they damage the life of others and are completely oblivious to this fact. But, in either case, the end result is the same, life lost.

Here is the space where a person's life becomes so forcefully defined by the actions of another that the only thought is the distaste for that other person. As we pass though life there will, no doubt, be times when this emotion is experienced by all of us. And, in most cases, we did not ask for, desire, or expect this life situation to happen. We did nothing to motivate the others person's actions. All we were doing was living our life. Yet, they are the one who forced their way into our existence.

If you have experienced this type of life event, what have you done while in the midst of it? Did you fight, yell, scream, or simply internalize it? In some cases there is nothing that you can really do. But still, there you are trapped by the words and actions of another and forced to exist in the space of life lost.

Obviously, getting away from these situations the moment they began to occur is the ideal option. But, that is not always possible. So, there you sit, life lost; hating the person or persons who is creating the problem, wishing them ill will, and feeling only a constant sense of anger.

The thing is, some people are very forgiving, some

people are very understanding – they try to look and see the root cause of the other person's motivation for them doing what they do. But, just as anger is an expressed emotion, based upon another person's actions, so too is compassion. Though you may feel one or the other, neither one of them ever replaces life lost. So, an emotion is never the answer.

In life, a minute turns into an hour, an hour into a day, a day into a year. Every second of life lost is gone. And, another person brought about that life lost. So yes, they are responsible. Yes, they will surfer the karma. But, it is still you who must embrace what they have set in motion as your moments of life tick by.

Metaphysically, we all, whether intentionally or not, reach to a logical resolution to these situations. If we are trapped, we try to move our mind to a space of tranquility and seek the silence within the noise. For if all we do is exist within a space of anger, then anger comes to be the defining factor of our life and we will move that anger forward onto others. And, this is never the ideal result.

So, what can you do with life lost? There is no absolute answer. But, try forming that lifetime/life space into a clear mental bubble and see it as encapsulated. Witness it as being separate from your actual being. See it outside of yourself. See the person or persons who motivated it locked inside of that bubble. See the moments of that period of lost life also there, outside of yourself. Make it a meditation. Clearly define it as something else. Let go of all the anger and place it in that bubble. Once that bubble is highly actualized watch it dissipate. Let it float off into space. Let it go out there into the ethos. Witness the person and/or persons dissolve. Allow all of any negative emotions attached to those peoples and that circumstance dissolve. Very consciously let it all go and emerge with a calmer, clearer state of mind.

At this point, it is time to take life action. Isolate who the person is and what they are doing to your life. Now, consciously chart a course of action that will cause them to stop creating life lost in your life space. Think it through clearly and take positive forceful action. Remember it is not only your future life space you are saving but that of others, as well. For if they have done what they have done to you, they will do it to other people. Save others as you save yourself. And, if you can't simply immediately leave the situation, fight the good fight until you have won.

If you decided that you are more than someone else. If you decided that you have the right to pass judgment on someone else. If you consciously or unconsciously alter the life of another person by setting a course of events in motion, expect to receive the consequences.

You have no right to take from someone else. You have no right to say things about someone else. You have no right to dominate the life of someone else with your actions either consciously or unconsciously. If you do, what do you expect will happen to you? Even if you feel empowered for the moment, if you hurt people, that empowerment will be very short lived.

Be better. Be more. Only say and do good things. And, always take the other person into consideration first.

* * *

03/March/2015 08:40 AM

    If you believe that you are something that someone else is not, you are lying to yourself.

* * *

03/March/2015 08:10 AM

    Surrender and become who and what you truly are. Not what you want to be, not what you think you should be, but what you truly are.

Letting Go of the Dream
03/March/2015 08:09 AM

Kind of building upon my previous blog, a lot of people find it very hard to let go of the dream(s) they possess for their life. This is true even when those dreams begin to damage their life. Like I have long semi-jokingly said, *"Everybody wants to be a movie star, don't they?"* But, the reality is, very few will ever reach that level of success.

The fact is, to achieve anything you have to try. Without trying, very little is ever obtained. But, you also have to keep a sharp focus on the reality of your life if you hope to not drive yourself into the madhouse or the poorhouse.

Like it is discussed in the metaphysical aspects of Hinduism, people have a thought and the more they think that thought the deeper that thought carves a ravine into their brain. The more it is thought of, the deeper it gets. And, the deeper the ravine, the harder it becomes to ever let it go.

This is also the case of desire. Whether it is a desire for a person, a thing, or a life career, the more you think about it, the more that desire becomes integrated into your being.

But, a desire is just a desire. It is what you want. But, it may not be what you can have. And, here is where so many people go wrong in their lives. They desire their desire and they do all they can do achieve their desire. Some go about achieving it through normal, accepted methods. Others lie, cheat, steal, hurt, and deceive in hopes of obtaining it. But, no matter what the actions, if the actions equal nothing, all they do is ultimate harm your life and the lives of those around you. It is for this reason that it is essential that you employee an astute sense of discretion in whatever you pursue. For if you don't, you may do something you can never recover from.

It is fine to have a desire. It is fine to go after your life dreams. This being said, you must also possess an internal gage that tells you when your desire will not be fulfilled and you must walk a different path.

In life, everybody wants to be something. They want to be something great. They hope to be seen as something great. This is simply a programmed aspect of human nature that has risen to prominence in the modern mind. It's not wrong, it just is. But, if you allow that mindset to dominate your existence you miss all the beauty and the perfection of the simple and the wholly whole.

To be free and to live a self-fulfilled life, you need to be able to let go of your desires when you realize that your desires are controlling you and you are not controlling them or when your desires are causing damage to the lives of other people.

Only you can do this. Stop being controlled by what you want to be. Stop pretending to be something you will never be. And, be whole in who you actually are.

When It Doesn't Work
02/March/2015 01:29 PM

So often I encounter people who are chasing whatever dream it is they are chasing but their world is falling down around them. I imagine that I frequently encounter these types of people because of the fact I live in L.A. L.A. where everyone seems to come chasing the promise of a dream. But, for all those who have found their dream here, there have been millions upon millions who have not.

Whether it is people chasing the dream of acting in or directing films, playing music, dancing, doing art, doing photography, writing a script or a book, owning a business, you name it... Very few of these people ever achieve their dreams.

I have watched so many people suffer, when their suffering was brought on by themselves. They have invested in equipment they can't afford, lied about their income to live in apartments or houses they can't afford, buy cars they can't afford so they can project an image of success, they pay for classes and headshots they can't afford, or they have maxed out their credit cards producing a movie that they either do not finish or cannot sell. You name it, I have seen it.

In fact, when the team that was publicizing Robert Rodriguez's *El Mariachi* was claiming that the film that made it into the theaters cost only $7,000.00 to create, I know several people who went bankrupt over believing that lie – thinking that they too could produce a film of that caliber for that amount of money. Who holds the karma for that?

And, that's just the thing... When someone who has hurt, lied to, or deceived people goes under, there is no emotion attached to their failure. They deserve it; right? But, when people go under when all they do is try to succeed, then another avenue of investigation needs to be viewed.

Certainly, we can say that all the people who try and fail are following a path of desire. And, as the Buddha so aptly stated, *"The cause of suffering is desire."* But, most people could care less about metaphysics. All they know and/or care about is the reality of what is right in front of their nose. They want to be something. But, the fact is, being something is almost impossible. Yet, so many people chase after it.

The people I witness failing always have one commonality. That commonality is that they do not investigate other pathways of survival. They are an actor, a filmmaking, an artist, a photographer, a dancer, an author – as they ARE, they can and should not have to be anything else. Wrong!

On a slightly different variant of this pathway, there are so many people that are financed by their families or they live under the roof of their family. The fact is, if you are an adult, over the age of eighteen, and you are either financed by and or living under the roof of your parents, and are not set about on a directed course of moving out onto your own, you are a failure. Just like the drug addicts and the alcoholics need to accept, the first thing you need to do is to admit to yourself you have a problem if you ever hope to get better. Face life! Get out on your own!

The people I see failing, particularly financially, do so because they never investigate a new course of action. The fact is, if what you are doing is not working; get a job! Yeah, it may not be what you want to do. Yeah, you may believe you are way more than that. But, the fact is, if you were, then you would be. As you are not, you are not.

The true reality of life; the true spirituality of life, is admitting to yourself and to the world that all you are, is what you are. You may have dreams but never let your dreams destroy you. For if you do, how do you come back from that?

Stop pretending. Stop spending money you don't have. Stop lying to others and particularly stop lying to yourself and do what it takes to survive. And, do it consciously, without lying to or hurting others. If that means getting a job, get one. Think of all the new experiences you will gain.

The true essence of life is living within your own perfection. Not trying to be something you are not but simply being something you are.

I Can Probably Use It Later
02/March/2015 01:27 PM

There was a massive rain and thunderstorm that passed through my area of L.A. this morning. I was all set to go out, as I love to drive in the rain, but I decided to stay home and listen to the rain on my roof, as it really is a magical experience.

When the rain subsided I headed out to get my breakfast on. I sat outside at the restaurant, as I always prefer to do, and was watching my day unfold.

There was this guy working on something in the back of the restaurant. As he walked by with his toolbox two twenty-something girls approached him and asked him if he had a wrench, as the license plate on their car was loose. He said he probably had something and they went inside. A few minutes later the two girls walked out with a crescent wrench. I watched as they tightened up their license plate. The girl whose car it was then looked at her friend, opened her truck, and put the wrench inside. She said, *"I can probably use it later."* They got in the car and drove off.

Obviously, this made me smile... A nice guy doing the right thing and loaning a wrench to a couple of semi-attractive girls. They left with his wrench. I hope he didn't need it for the job he was doing. ☺

Arrogance and Oblivion
01/March/2015 09:10 AM

A person's life is defined by a person's actions. The cumulative effect of what a person has done is what they are seen to be by the world. A person can lie about whom they are – they can claim to be something they are not, but at the end of a person's life all they truly will be defined by is solely interpreted by what they have done.

As we pass through life we each encounter the various types of personalities. We encounter those who are truly giving, truly care, and are nice. We also encounter those who are selfish, unthinking, and uncaring about anyone but himself or herself. When we encounter these types of people, the question often arises in our mind, *"Why does a person behave in this manner?"* Commonly, the answer is arrogance or oblivion.

People project the quality of arrogance for many reasons. Perhaps they come from a family that holds a lot of money or perhaps they have earned a lot of money themselves. With this, they then believe that their money provides them with a better placement in life and all others are not of their equal. Arrogance also can be witnessed, especially in the young, when a person has the unrelenting support of their family who finances their lifestyle and pays for their desires. Here, arrogance is based on a somewhat different set of criteria. For this person, arrogance comes from a mindset of not self-wholeness, but of the young cub being protected by the mama bear. They are not whole onto themselves but they believe from the power of their family, they are protected and are, thereby, somehow more. This same state of mind is also the sourcepoint for the arrogance of one who is surround by a strong group of friend; be it a team, a gang, a fraternity, or how ever else people congregate in groups. Once accepted inside that group, the person not only believes they are protected by that group but they try to push the boundaries of who and what they are by exhibiting bad, negative, or arrogant behavior, based on that's group mentality, in order to cement their placement in the congregation.

On the other side of the spectrum, arrogance is also commonly based upon a person's individualized insecurity. If a person has not personally accomplished anything with their life, there are those who possess a specific psychological makeup that turns to arrogance as a defense mechanism. This type of person may see the lives of those who have succeeded and unconsciously deduce that the only they way they can equal the life fullness of others is to behave in the manner of those who have achieved wealth, fame, success, love, and strong friendships. From this, a person who embraces this mindset projects a misguided sense of arrogance based upon personal deception that is then projected out to the world.

From arrogance, a lot of bad things have happened to people in life. I believe if we look back through our own personal life interactions we can each remember some negative occurrence that happened to us based upon a person's arrogance, maybe even our own.

The other debilitating life definition comes about due to a person behaving in an oblivious manner. Think about this, *"How many times has something negative occurred in your life and it was brought about due to the unconscious, oblivious actions of another person?"* No matter how many times a person denies their actions or claims, *"I didn't know,"* or *"I didn't understand,"* that never undoes the damage that they have brought to your life.

Personal oblivion is brought about by several factors in a person's life. It may, in fact, be brought about by arrogance. For example, a person is so self-involved that they do not think about others. But, more often it occurs simply due to an individual being locked so deeply into their own mind, thinking only about what they want to think about – thinking only about themselves and their own desires that they do not take the time to take others into consideration before they do what they do. I believe we will each state, *"This is not the place that a person should be living their life from."* But, think how many people behave in just that manner.

At the root of all life is you. You are the sourcepoint for your life and your world. How you behave in your life sets the standard for not only how you will be defined but how others may come to learn from you. Learn, not from your words but your actions. For the truth be told, words mean very little. People can say anything they want; they can speak the truth or they can lie. But, actions are the defining factor of all life. To this end, put away arrogance. Become super conscious instead of oblivious and be the essence of good.

Do You Step On Snails?
26/February/2015 09:09 AM

I think that most of us, since the time we were children, have seen the many aspects of life around us. Whether it was the seashells at the beach, which are now very few and far between, or the butterflies flying through the air, which have also diminished greatly, we see and appreciate the beauty of nature.

There are other forms of life that some people do not take note of and/or do not particularly like. Snails, for example. Yeah, they are kind of weird. But, they are also beautiful and an integral part of our biosphere.

I remember as a kid, some people I knew would intentionally step on them. That made just a yucky mess. Even way back then I thought that was a very wrong thing to do. Now, whenever I see a snail I have a great appreciation for its purpose and placement in life.

Whenever it rains here in L.A., snails come out to play. They move onto the sidewalks. Whenever I see them I tell them to be careful. I tell them to be careful because so many people are so unconscious or so full of the nothing that they believe they are that they do not even take the time to study where they are stepping and they smash them. Not only is it wrong to unnecessarily kill essential life but also it is wrong to be that unconscious of where you are walking.

This is the thing about human life, and perhaps its biggest downfall, people don't care. And, they do not care that they don't care. They are so wrapped up in their own superiorness, or in whatever is going on in their ego driven mind, that they do not take the time to study where and how they walk. This is very sad. Snails get killed.

If you are passing though life not caring and not being acutely aware of your environment, what does that say about you? If you don't care, should anyone or anything care about you?

Being conscious, being caring is the sourcepoint of living a good, fulfilled, and giving life. Do you study where you step?

*   *   *

26/February/2015 08:47 AM

If you are looking for the source-point of the karma, the person responsible is the person who set the course of events in motion.

* * *

26/February/2015 08:46 AM

Do you care if what you do hurts someone else?

If you do, that defines the person you are.

If you do not, that also defines the person you are.

Which type of person do you believe is better?

Abandoned in the Moment
25/February/2015 04:45 PM

A passage from one of my books that I am told a lot of people quote on twitter is, *"Take the time to just do nothing. It will open up a completely new world of insight for you."* I truly believe this... That people really need to STOP, step back, and do absolutely nothing periodically in their life.

It's not easy, I know. Me too... I am such an ON person that it is very difficult for me to STOP and do nothing. But, when I do, I truly see the benefit.

It's important to note that, *"Doing nothing,"* is not the same a meditating. Meditating is doing something. But, doing nothing is doing nothing.

Most people when they chill, instead of doing nothing, they listen to music, read a book, watch TV, surf the web, or whatever... Or, they may take a nap. But, this is all different from consciously doing nothing. Doing nothing is doing nothing. You must simply sit back or lie down, and let yourself BE.

There is no absolute technique in this practice. It is for you to design of your own accord. The main thing to not let happen, however, is to not let your mind drift to things, situation, or interactions with people that made you angry. For if your mind goes to those life moments then all you will do is find yourself being upset. Again, that is not doing nothing, being upset is doing something.

One of the things that I have noticed often times happens to me whenever I STOP is that quite often I find that something will try to distract me. Maybe it is a car alarm outside, a person talking loudly, or, like today, a small gnat that decided to fly around my face. I jokingly say to myself when these types of things occur, "I'm just being tested." Because it is very hard to STOP when you are flapping your hands trying to get a gnat to leave you alone. ☺ But, you really need to do whatever it takes to get yourself in a silent space and let go. Maybe that is wearing noise-canceling headphone or something like that. Maybe you are not a city dweller and then silence is much more closely at hand. But, whatever it takes, let yourself fall into that ZERO SPACE as often as you can.

"Take the time to just do nothing. It will open up a completely new world of insight for you."

* * *

25/February/2015 04:20 PM

    What does confrontation equal? Just another fight that you either win or lose.

* * *

25/February/2015 08:55 AM

If you are looking for something that doesn't exist you can spend your whole lifetime searching and never find it.

The Metaphysics of Driving
24/February/2015 05:06 PM

Driving a car or a motorcycle is one of the most dangerous things that you can do. Think about it, going down the freeway, at the speed cars drive at, you could get in an accident and be killed at any moment. It happens all the time. But, people never think about this. They just drive. They want to get there from here... And, that is that.

Driving can also be a very metaphysical experience if you tune into another stage of consciousness. I mean, have you ever been driving a long and it just seems like all of the cars get out of your way, just as you need be going where you need to go?

Now, I am not about magical thinking on any level. I find it very deceptive. But, I also study the patterns of life. For example, in the latter years of when I used to operate a martial art studio, I lived in Hermosa Beach but my studio was in Reseda, which is in the San Fernando Valley. Every afternoon I would get in my *'64 Porsche 356 SC* and have to head out and onto the 405 freeway, (which is known to be a mess), and drive from the beach to the valley. But, as time progressed, I realized that if I really got into my moment, remained very conscious, I could literally anticipate the movements of the cars ahead of me and get to my destination in a very precise and rapid manner.

What metaphysically went on is very hard to put into words. But, I can say, next time you are driving and you need to be somewhere, instead of spacing out on the music, checking your texts, replaying past events in your mind, or thinking about whom you love or whom you hate, get focused. Get your mind in the moment and you may be amazed at what will occur during your driving experience.

On a more simply level, we can look at the metaphysics of driving in a more concrete manner. Think about this, as I am sure it has happened to all of us. You are driving; a car selfishly or recklessly cuts you off and pulls in front of you. By them doing what they did, it messes everything up. Another car pulls in; you miss the stoplight and have to wait or by them doing what they did, a whole batch of traffic gets in your way and you are frustratingly held back from reaching your destination in an expedient manner.

The thing is, sometimes just the opposite happens. People get out of our way and a passageway opens up and we just drive straight on through. But, these times, we don't think about. It is the times when another driver causes us frustration and our blood pressure goes up that we remember. We honk. We scream. We give people the bird. All in the life of driving… ☺

But, the point I am trying to make here is… All of life has a pattern and a flow. Each life event and each segment in life has its own unique pattern and flow. If you can just get conscious enough to study it and move within it, then a whole new world of understanding opens up to you.

Try it. See what happens.

Where You Place Yourself
24/February/2015 05:03 PM

Where you initially find yourself in life is not your fault or your creation. We are each born where we are born.

When we are young we are defined by our surroundings. If where you find yourself is nice, good, and nurturing, then your life and your mind is provided with the ability to expand, interact, learn, and grow. If, on the other hand, you initially find yourself surrounded by a stifling environment, it will be hard to become all that you can be.

We each want something from our life. We each want something for our life. The question you must initially ask yourself is, *"Why do I want what I want?"* For without a concise definition for that query, all life just becomes happenstance. But, once you know the answer to that question, it is only you, as your progress into adult, who can consciously take and make the actions that will get you to where you want to be.

Many people, due to the accident of birth find themselves born into a debilitating geography or sociological space. They are not provided with what they need to grow. Many people, even though they know that what they truly want is out there, (not in here), stay in the environment where they were born. From this, they become defined by all of the limitation of their limited life space.

It is essential to understand, this is not a criticism, it is simply a statement of fact. Moving away from the nest can be hard. It is also difficult to break free from all of the social and psychological programming one receives via where they grow up. For the most part, people mentally integrate into their surrounding atmosphere rather than to rebel against it. They conform rather than reform.

All this being stated, if you have a vision for your life; if you want to grow and you know that you cannot reach your full potential where you currently find yourself, it must be you who takes the initiative to get yourself where you need to be so you can be stimulated with the right influences to live the life you dream of.

Nothing Noteworthy
24/February/2015 05:02 PM

I always find it curious when people go out of their way to critique the life, life actions, and or doings of another person. There are some people who, in fact, spend their whole life doing this.

People speak their mind on their phone, friend-to-friend, on various internet sites, on social media, and the list goes on. They talk and talk, write and write, but the ultimate question has to be, *"What does all this equal?"* If you spend your Life-Time talking about the doings of others, what are you doing?

You know, it doesn't really matter if you go out of your way to say something nice. Or, as most, *"Talkers,"* do say something negative, for the ultimate essence of your equation is that; one: all you are doing is talking and two: you most likely don't know what you're talking about.

People base all of their opinions upon a very limited set of facts. From this they spread their message to the masses. But, what you think is not what another person thinks, just as what you are proclaiming may most probably be completely wrong. But, who is there to judge the judger.

The people who speak the most loudly are rarely the ones to do anything of consequence in their life. They do not create the creations, they do not provide a service via a business, they do not donate their time to help the greater good. All they do is discus the life and the actions of others.

Go anywhere, in any public place. Stop. Listen to the words being spoken around you. How many of them are discussing the life and the doings of others? I believe many of them will be doing just that. Do you?

True life, true-life contribution is about the doing, the creating, not the discussing what someone else has done or has created. Stop discussing and critiquing the works, the words, and the lives of others or all you will be left with at the end of your days is meaningless dribble – start making your own contribution(s).

*   *   *

22/February/2015 06:41 PM

    If you care enough to care then there will never be the necessity to make an excuse for what you have done.

*　　*　　*

22/February/2015 06:37 PM

If you change the truth to a lie then all of life becomes murky and convoluted.

* * *

22/February/2015 06:34 PM

    People prefer to live their lives oblivious to the needs of others.

    Why?

    Because it is easier to only care about one's self.

*   *   *

22/February/2015 06:33 PM

Why does someone become mad at you?

Because you have done something wrong.

*   *   *

22/February/2015 06:33 PM

    Anything that you do that hurts another person is done from the mindset of selfishness.

* * *

22/February/2015 09:09 AM

Your life is defined by the bad things you have done not by the good things you have done.

* * *

22/February/2015 09:06 AM

If what you do affects anyone it affects everyone.

* * *

22/February/2015 09:05 AM

Why does a person become religious?

>Is it so they can say, *"I am but you are not?"*

Style Over Substance or Substance Over Style
22/February/2015 09:01 AM

As I have long detailed, very few people hold onto any sense of style as they move into adulthood. When a person is a teenager, and some even into their early twenties, their personal definition of style is very important to them. But, as age and the responsibilities of life move to the forefront, personal style is quite commonly lost.

Yesterday, we were kickin' around the great grouping of antique stores that exist in Orange, California. As soon as we arrived I noticed this one couple that pretty much paralleled our movements from store to store. The guy he was noticeable tall, maybe six foot-eight with very long hair sprouting a grey streak. His lady wore a pair of those knee-high *Demonia* boots with six-inch platforms. They were obviously Goths. Their age was probably in their early forties.

So here it was, a couple who balked a society and lived what they lived by their own sense of definition. They maintained their style well into their middle age.

Personally, I always have an appreciation for people who do that, whatever their unique style may be, for they are so few and far between. But, then the second question arises, who are they on parade for? For that is exactly what they are doing. They are saying, *"Here, look at me."* For the abnormal always stands apart from the norm and, as such, all eyes go to them.

This is also the thing about, *"Forced- Spirituality,"* as I have titled it. Those who play dress-up in their robes and their collars or the funeral ash smeared all over their body. *"Here, look at me, I am holy."* But, are they? Do the truly holy play dress-up or are the truly holy silent with in and with out themselves?

Life is truly about who and what you are. How do you see yourself? How do you project that to the world? Does your projection project the necessary you? Or, are you simply trying to play dress-up to become a comic book character?

Who Are You To Know?
21/February/2015 09:10 AM

The internet never lies; does it?

That is the ongoing joke about how much misinformation about people, places, and things is put out there on the internet all the time. People write all kinds of nonsense about what they believe, based on nothing more than their own beliefs. As wrong as this is, that is the way it is.

On the other side of the issue some people put out way too much TMI. They tell the all and the everything about what they are feeling and what they are living through.

I think about this one girl that I know via Facebook. She has spelled out her whole breakup with this guy on Facebook. I imagine that there is some emotional cleanings going on by presenting her feelings and getting them out there but what she has also done is to let a whole world of people, (people like me who don't really know her), into the inner workings of her mind. Good or bad? I don't know? But, it is what it is. And, that is the way it is with many people.

The thing is, even in situations like this, where the girl spelled it out, there is still only the inner part of her that is truly in touch with what is going on in her mind and her heart. Yet, everyone who reads her story attaches their own set of judgments to her trails and tribulations.

People what to judge. Some do this much more other. Some people allow others to feel what they feel, write what they write, and let that be the end of it. Others, what to pick apart people words so they can find a way to attach their own judgment to their words. These are the people who are not whole onto themselves as they must go to the words and works of other people to find a way to give themselves a sense of purpose.

Ultimately, no matter what you may think you know about a person; you know, (at best), very little. You are not in their mind. Thus, you should never pass judgment on the words or thoughts of another individual for if you do all you have done is diminish your own self worth by looking to someone else to find a reason to be.

*   *   *

21/February/2015 08:45 AM

Which is better:
      caring or not caring,
      being oblivious or being hyperaware,
      being selfish or selfless,
      giving or taking,
      consideration or confrontation?

* * *

20/February/2015 09:19 AM

Do you associate with people who tell you what you want to hear or do you associate with people who tell you the truth?

In the Dog House
20/February/2015 08:53 AM

There was this very sad scene present on the news last night. Somebody had apparently made this rag tag doghouse and nailed their dog inside of it. Because they did this in such a crappy area, it took the police three days to care enough to look inside. What they found was this beaten and bitten poor dog cowering in the back of the doghouse. When the animal control people came to remove him, he resisted, as he didn't know what was going on, but he didn't bite, bark, or growl. Obviously, a sweet dog.

The dog was taken to a shelter where he is being given medical treatment and will be rehabilitated and eventually adopted out to a new home. Thank god for organizations that do stuff like that instead of simply putting animals to sleep!

For most of us we question, *"How could anyone do that to their dog?"* But, the fact is, people are bad. There are a lot of bad people out there. They abuse their animals, other people, themselves, and life in general. I have watched people scold their dogs with a belt, smack their cats around like they are nothing, declaw their cats – shame on you!

If you have ever had a pet you know that each dog, cat, bunny, hamster, fish, whatever, has their own unique personality. They are whole and all onto themselves. They are life. And, all life deserves respect. They are not simply something to take out your frustrations upon, use as a punching bag, or believe that they are anything less than something great.

All life is life and every person, animal, and all things matter. The moment you can care enough about caring and turn your own foolish dominate mentality off and realize this, everything becomes better.

Care!

Ego Over Ability
20/February/2015 08:39 AM

How many people have you met that tell you all of the great things they are going to do someday? But, someday comes and they have done nothing.

How many people have you met that tell you all of the things they can do better than someone else? They sit, analyze, make comments, brag, and criticize but they personally never accomplish anything.

Some people do step up to the plate and try to do what they want to do. In this modern world they may have a website stating their abilities, they may Facebook, tweet, instagram, and do all the social media necessities. But, their claims of ability do not equal their actual ability, so when push comes to shove all they are doing is feeding their own ego. They ultimately provided No One with No Thing.

People really should be honest with themselves. They should analyze their life desires and put them in context to their actual life abilities. I realize this is a pipe dream as most people are not that self-inquisitive. But, think how much better the world would be if people stopped lying to themselves, lying to the world, and spouting out all of the nonsense that pollutes this life space.

* * *

20/February/2015 08:28 AM

If you don't acknowledge your crime, your crime becomes criminal.

* * *

20/February/2015 08:27 AM

Do you know when enough is enough?

* * *

20/February/2015 08:26 AM

If you do not undo any damage you create that damage will come to define you.

* * *

18/February/2015 02:06 PM

Personally deciding that you are something does not make you something. It is only when other people proclaim that you are something that you become that which they proclaim.

Hipsters in a Crosswalk
18/February/2015 02:05 PM

I was over in Echo Park today. The actually Echo Park is one of those old, now remodeled, junkyard parks that inhabit the ancient landscape of L.A. near downtown. You can see it in a few of my Zen Films; i.e. *Undercover X.*

Anyway, I was waiting to turn left to go towards the 101. There is this big crosswalk that goes from the park over to the old apartment buildings that line the street. In the crosswalk there were four hipsters, three men and one girl, all with the same hipster haircuts and the same nasty hipster beards, (except the girl, of course). They were walking in the crosswalk way slower than any one should ever be allowed to walk. They slowly meandered and smoked while the line of cars built up behind me.

One guy in a pickup truck must have said, *"Fuck it,"* and he drove out and around them. A moment or two later, the car in front of me, filled with Latin bangers drove through the intersection behind them. The guy in the passenger seat, while yelling something at them in Spanish, through what appeared to be about half of a Subway sandwich and hit the redheaded hipster right in the backside of his face. The hipsters all turned around about to say something but then they took at look at who had done it and they said nothing. They're lucky they didn't get shot.

There the guy stood, lettuce and mayo dripping from his nasty beard. I drove by and smiled.

Now normally, I am not in favor of that style of civil disobedience. But, these assholes deserved it. As all people who take up the Life-Time and Life-Space of other people, for no reason, deserved to be smacked in the face with a Subway sandwich. ☺

Things That You Think You Know
18/February/2015 08:23 AM

Have you ever had the experience of believe that you knew something and then some time later finding out that you were completely wrong? Maybe this was believing that you knew a certain fact and it turned out to be wrong. Maybe it was believing in a person and they turned out to be wrong. Maybe it was believing in a religious ideology and it turned out to be wrong. Whatever it was, didn't you feel pretty stupid when you finally realized the truth?

I think back to when I was in my typing class at *Virgil Junior High School*. It was right at the time when the band *Steely Dan* was hitting the charts with their song, *"Do it Again."* The guy sitting next to me and I were discussing the song, as teenagers tend to do. The thing was, this guy swore that the name of the band was, *"Do it Again,"* and the song was, *"Steely Dan."* I tried to explain to him that he was wrong but I truly had never met anyone so adamant in their belief. One part of me wanted him to know the truth. The other part realized that it was better to just let it go and let the guy believe whatever it was he wanted.

This is the thing about belief; there are some who are open to hearing new thoughts, ideas, and facts, and then altering their thought process when new information is presented to them. Many people are not like this, however, when they <u>believe</u> they <u>believe</u> and that is that.

As we pass though life we will each meet people like this. In many cases, to argue with them is pointless, because whether it is the name of a band or a religious ideology there is no way to alter their mind and direct it towards the truth.

And, this is the thing about the truth, what is it? In most cases, the truth is only something that we believe but through time, science, and human evolution that understanding changes.

Possessing an open mind is a boon in life. It keeps you clear of conflict and provides you with an ever expanding understanding of, if nothing else, human psychological behavior. Just as what the marital arts took from the ways of nature and teaches us, it is better to deflect and bend then to meet force with force, this too is the case of life. Being subtle keeps you free flowing. Being a rock keeps you from ever moving, changing your location, and/or learning anything new. Don't be stuck!

* * *

18/February/2015 12:10 AM

When did you learn to say the things you say?

* * *

18/February/2015 12:09 AM

    Do people love you?

        If they do ask yourself, why?

    Do people hate you.

        If they do ask yourself, why?

*   *   *

18/February/2015 12:09 AM

What are you going to become?

* * *

17/February/2015 08:35 AM

    The options you choose from are defined by the options that you believe you have.

* * *

16/February/2015 02:15 PM

    The only time you are allowed in is when you ask to be invited in. Whatever happens after that point becomes your fault.

* * *

16/February/2015 02:13 PM

    If you are not thinking about others before you think about yourself you are committing a sin against humanity.

* * *

16/February/2015 01:57 PM

How many times have you made the same mistake?

* * *

16/February/2015 01:56 PM

How many people are at fault but try to blame others for their own actions?

When You Do Something Bad
16/February/2015 10:09 AM

Bad things go on all around us. There are the *Big Bads* like war, people who intentionally hurt other people, people who don't think or care about the damage they are creating and then there are the *Little Bads;* small mistakes, white lies, and minor accidents.

Sometimes the *Little Bads* become the *Big Bads.* Your *Little Bad* can lead to your *Big Bad.* For example, you do something wrong to someone or something. Then, instead of saying, *"Sorry,"* you blame the other person. An example could be a person isn't paying attention to their environment, they do bad things and behave in a bad way and damage the life space of others. Maybe, someone isn't looking and they cause an accident with you car. Then, instead of owning it, they get mad at you, they try to turn it around on you, and the list goes on. *Little Bads* can give birth to *Big Bads* because things can escalate. If someone doesn't own, change, or fix their actions, then anger is given birth to. And, anger (even one person's anger) can give birth to all out war.

It is really important that you study what you do. It is really essential that you care about the affect you are having on others. It is really elemental that if you do a *Little Bad* you stop it, take responsibility for it, and fix it before it becomes a *Big Bad.*

In life, we are surround by all types of people. There are the nice people, which we hope to be surround by, but there are also the arrogant, the deceitful, the angry, and the misguided. These are the people that lead to life problems.

Though we do not wish for them to be in our life space, there is no doubt that we are going to encounter them.

So, just Be More. You personally, Be More! Do only Good Things. And, if you do something wrong, a *Little Bad*, stop thinking about yourself, and do more Good than the damage the *Little Bad* created and choose to make things better for all.

Explanations About What We Do and Do Not Know
16/February/2015 10:08 AM

I was joking around with a friend of mine about our time at the university. She was always one of those really good students. Me, not so much. My life was always lived outside of school.

She discussed how she used to always do extra credit assignments to be sure to keep a really high GPA. Me, I laughingly told her I had only done one.

I had this course on cartography where we viewed and drew maps. The thing was, the course was based around studying maps through these 3D glasses. Though the instructor and the students talked about all of this jumping off the page effect, I couldn't see it. What I didn't know at the time was that I can't see traditional 3D images on maps, in the movies, or otherwise. I later found out this is because I have one eye that sees so much worse than the other one, due to being hit by a Japanese gardener's truck, while riding my bike, the day before my eighth birthday and having my face; i.e. my eye hit the curb.

So, I was terrible at that class. The only thing that saved me was that there was an extra credit calligraphy assignment; as calligraphy is also a part of map creation. By that point in my life I was really good at calligraphy. So, as the instructor told me, that was the only thing that saved me.

I never explained to the instructor that I couldn't see what I was supposed to be seeing. I guess I didn't really get it. I didn't know, because I couldn't know, as no one told be that there were people like me.

And, here is one of the big things about life and about life definitions, and who and what we become. We only know what we know. We only know what we are taught. We only know what is explained to us. From there, only then is it us who can decide to do what we do with that information.

Some people do good things with the information they are presented with. Others do not. But, if you don't know, you don't know.

Some people are very busy spouting off all that they think they know to the world. They hear or they learn something and then they want to broadcast it to make themselves seem like some kind of all-knowing figure. I believe we have each met people like that, know-it-alls. Others learn and know things but they keep the knowledge deep within, only expressing it if asked or if it is required to move something positive along in life.

But, the ultimate truth of life is, if you don't know you don't know. If you know, then you know, but then what? Most of life is lived via a speculative, ideology based upon a system of opinions. Facts are facts but life is driven forward by personal philosophy.

Which way do you live your life, by fact or by fiction?

* * *

16/February/2015 09:51 AM

You are the reason for everything that is happening in your life, both good and bad. Look to the source-point and you will know the reason why.

* * *

16/February/2015 09:51 AM

Just because somebody says that they are going to do something does not mean that they will do something.

Happy Valentine's Day 2015
15/February/2015 09:07 AM

It was a warm Valentine's Day here in L.A. Maybe fifteen degrees above normal. My lady and I were coming home after checking out some coastal cliff locations for an upcoming shoot. As we were coming up the hill there was a major traffic jam of cars, which never occurs in this area. As we approached, right at the end of our street, we see that a motorcycle was down and in pieces. It had been hit by a car turning left.

The same thing happened to me back in '79. It was a warm summer afternoon and I hopped on my scoot and was heading over to my mother's place in Hollywood for Sunday night dinner. BAM a girl turned left into me, hit me, and sent me face first into the pavement. For the first few days they thought I was gone. But, after they pulled my skull off of my frontal lobe, cauterized the blood clots in my brain, pinned by face back together, I made it. Made it, but my body, face, and mind were never the same again.

If you ride a motorcycle, and I still do (sometimes), it is not if you are going to get into an accident, it is when. And, it is virtually never the fault of the motorcycle rider.

As for this rider, they had already taken him away in an ambulance. But, looking at the condition of his bike, as it was totally in pieces, I know it was bad. Maybe he and his lady were out for a Valentine's Day ride, I don't know? But, I can only hope for the best, as he or they had to be in very bad shape.

As I passed the accident scene, as we had to go up and around and enter our neighborhood from a different street, I could see how most people didn't care at all about the accident victim(s). They were pissed about the hold up. They didn't care about the person or persons who got creamed by the SUV.

Now, this is how most people encounter life. They only care about themselves and they could care less about the pain of others. Are you like this? Do you care about the suffering of other people?

Think about all the carnage that is going on around the world right now, brought about militant or government groups in The Ukraine, Syria, Iraq, and Nigeria. Whether you agree with the policies of these groups or not isn't the issue. How many innocent people are having their lives ruined by the actions of other people? How many people have their lives ruined by the gangs or thugs in urban centers every day? The one common dominator of all this pain and suffering is that a person or people are <u>choosing</u> to do it.

Life ruination does not only take place on a global scale brought about by formalized groups, it is also on a person-to-person basis, as well. People hurt people, one-on-one, all they time. Not only in the aforementioned case of the motorcycle accident, but people choose to do things that will knowingly hurt other people. Some people do this consciously. They set about on a path to hurt someone and this can take place in so many ways. Have you done that?

The damaging of another person's life also takes place by unconscious or selfish actions. Have you hurt someone's life and either did not notice or did not care?

The thing is, most people operate from a very selfish perspective. They behave like the driver's pasting the accident scene. They didn't care about the victims. They only cared about how much time it was costing them to pass by. Do you live your life in that manner?

Have you had someone either consciously or unconsciously damage your life? Have you done it to others?

The only thing I can say in all of this is that to make anything better in this life-place you really need to be more conscious and less selfish. You really need to think about others and care about others. Doesn't it make you feel better when someone takes the time to care about you? Doesn't it make you feel worse when someone messes with your life?

If you are hurting someone, stop it! Undo and fix what you have done!

If you are presented with a choice in the future to help or to hurt, always choose to help. Help till it hurts! Then, all of life becomes better; not only for you but for everyone else, as well.

If you help, people love you. If you hurt, people hate you. Which do you think is better?

Who Know What is True?
15/February/2015 09:00 AM

One of the sad truths of life is you can never be sure that a person is telling you the truth. People misrepresent themselves all the time, they pretend to be something they are not, they have done things that they want no one to know about, so they hide their previous doings, or they say they are something/can do something when they cannot. Moreover, many people just flat out lie.

In life, we each try to surround ourselves with people we can believe and believe in. But, here too lies one of the problems. We want to believe in people. So, in many cases we give them the befit of the doubt. But then, if we find out that they are a deceiver it is oftentimes way too late for they have done damage to our lives.

Have you ever been lied to? Have you ever known a liar? Are you one?

Have you ever believed in someone only to find out much farther down the road that they were not who the claimed to be? Have you ever behaved in that fashion?

The truth is, if a person is willing to lie to you they do not care about the consequences. All they care about is obtaining whatever it is they believe they will obtain by orchestrating the lie. So, even if they are caught in the lie farther down the line, they have most commonly already obtained what they hoped to achieve.

There is no court of law for liars. If they are caught, they simply move onto their next believing victim.

The truth is the truth is the truth and that is that.

Too Old To Be Cool
15/February/2015 08:58 AM

I believe most people pass though life being age appropriate. They do what they do at the appropriate time of their physical evolution and they let go of the trappings of youth as they pass beyond that stage of life. Some people are not like that, however. They try to hang on tightly to youth when it is long gone by.

Every now an then you see one of these people. Female octogenarians with their hair dyed platinum blonde, wearing a miniskirt, with their arms all inked up, aging rockers wearing super tight jeans, a leather motorcycle jacket, with their long stringy hair flopping in the wind, and the deep lines of age cutting into their face, the aging punk rock sweetheart who still keeps her pink mohawk, the old guy who goes to restaurants and tries to pickup on the young waitresses just because the smile at him, or they old dude who always makes a play for the young and the beautiful. Dude, if you ain't a billionaire or Hugh Hefner, you got no shot!

Many people lived the best years of their life in their early days. They had fun, partied; experienced new and exciting events. And, that is the way it should be. That is what youth is for. But, the truth about life is that you can't go back. Yes, you can still have fun, do and experience fun and new things, but you should not try to be something you are not while you are doing them; i.e., young. For then, all you become is a joke.

Be whom you are when you are.

How Are You Defined By Other?
15/February/2015 08:55 AM

As I forever, semi jokingly state, *"Life is a complied mess."* But, within that complicated mess we must each try to etch out our own unique placement within life.

In life, it is not just us. In life we are surrounded by people: people we live with, people we know, people we don't know, people we work with, our neighbors, our friends, our enemies, people we love, and people we hate. In many cases, each of these people come to affect various elements of our lives.

There are those people who truly take other people into consideration before they do anything. Then, there are those who bulldoze their way through life, thinking of no one else but themselves, and attempt to dominate all space they inhabit. I believe we each know which of these personalities is better and which of these personalities is worse, but this does not change the fact that we must interact with all types of people as we pass through our existence.

Like I have long said, *"Who surrounds you, comes to define you."* But, to truly understand this ideology we must look more deeply into its meaning.

In life, few of us have the opportunity to completely orchestrate who will be allowed to be around us. I believe we each try to do that to varying degrees. We like the people we like. We don't like people we don't like. From this equation we try to only associate with the people we like. But, beyond all that there are the people we are forced to interact with; be they family members, workmates, or neighbors. In some cases, these are people we simply do not want to be around but we are forced to interact with them to varying degrees.

Most people are very simply in their choice of friends. If a person is nice, then it is fine to associate with them. But, if they are not, and we are forced to be anywhere near the presence of a person we don't like, this is where life evolution becomes not only stagnated but also possibly damaged by that individual.

The thing is, nice people are nice. They want to be nice. They do good things. They do not set about to damage anyone or anything thing. The people on the other side of the spectrum, however, are the selfish, the self-involved, the egotistical, the non-caring, the breed that lives in a constant state of deception and denial. These people do damage to the lives of all those they interact with and oftentimes do not even care.

Avoidance is perhaps the best philosophy when dealing with this type of individual. But, for any of us who have been forced to deal with people of this nature we understand, they always seem to find a way to infiltrate our lives. They may do this consciously, they may do this unconsciously, but the end result is the same, they have altered our positive life evolution.

There are those, when push comes to shove, who take aggressive actions to remove these people from their lives; some even resort to physical violence. But, by guiding your life in that direction what you have done is to allow the negativity that the aforementioned person possesses to dominate your being and send your life down a pathway that embraces all that is wrong with the world.

I believe that this is what many people who embrace that negative mindset desire – they hope to bring good people down to their negative level of life existence for then, they gain the power that they seek. ...The power that should come from the divine internal understanding of life and cosmic interaction but instead is lost to a world dominated by emotions and misplaced desires.

Now, I am not saying that action should not be taken if this type of person pushes your life up against the wall. What I am saying is that you must keep the YOU, YOU. Control your response(s) and find a way to redirect their negative actions in a manner that alleviates the problem without you being forced to be diminished to their level.

There is no one answer for this or I would pass it along to you. The thing to do is to truly evaluate your situation and find a way to disable their negative actions without the need for formal confrontation. But, if it does come to that, knock 'em out. ☺

Hope Less Kill More
13/February/2015 02:34 PM

I was down by the water today. It is an insanely hot day for February in L.A. So, there were tons of people on the sand. Me, I have long thought that I am probably better suited for some place like Seattle rather than L.A., as I love the rain but dislike the heat and the sun. Anyway...

As I was standing there watching the waves, this girl walks by wearing a tee shirt that said, *"Hope Less,"* on the frond and, *"Kill More,"* on the back. She had one of those total punk rock scowls on her face. Her and tee shirt made me smile.

"Hope Less," that saying is kind of metaphysical if you think about it. I mean so many people spend so much of their life, hoping... Hoping for a better life, a better job, a better car, a better place to live, a better relationship, more money, you name it. I mean people pray day in and day out hoping that by doing so their life will get better. If it does, all good. If it doesn't, then god is testing them or they don't deserve it.

People put all of these self-imposed definitions on their life as they hope and dream everything will get better. I don't know, have you ever prayed for and received what you ask for? If you did, once you had it, was it all you dreamt of?

"Kill More," that is kind of a hardcore saying. But, I think if we turn it around just a little bit, we can make it something more than it sounds. Kill the desire, then you are free. If you are whole and happy in all that you already have, than what more can you hope for?

Freedom is easy if you look for it in the right place.

Anyway, thanks Miss, *"Hope Less,"* Punk Rock girl. You made me smile and set me to thinking...

Somebody Must've Died
13/February/2015 08:39 AM

My local library has a great used bookstore. The way it works is that people donate books and then they put them out for sale. From this, there is a great cross section of subjects that they have to offer.

By my early thirties I had developed this massive library, literally thousands of books. It was crazy. I eventually moved most of them along. Now, every couple of years I go through my books and donate many of them to this library. Just recently I gave them well over a hundred books.

A couple of days after my donation I went in to see what new books they had to offer. Amusingly, I heard one of the people discussing several of the titles I had donated. She concluded, due to the large collection I gave them, *"Somebody must've died."* This, of course, made me smile. Dead? No, not yet. ☺

This is the thing about life; many of us make our life definitions based not upon fact but simply speculation. Many people define their entire reality based upon their assumptions. They have no facts, yet they believe what they think to be true and then they spread their ideologies to the world. Do you do this?

In life, you can think anything you want. Most of us reach our conclusions by researching the facts, studying a subject or the behavior of a person or persons, and then coming to a conclusion based upon the available data. Other people are not like this, however, they simply decide the way it is and then, to them, their undefined thoughts become fact. For those of us who seek the provable truth, this style of analysis tends to make us question the reality of any belief. For if a conclusion is not based upon provable facts and verifiable evidence then all of this reality becomes nothing more than a projection of an individual's preconceived notions.

You can think whatever you want. You can believe whatever you want. But, before you announce your thoughts or speculative conclusions to the world it is probably best to not base your spoken truths upon speculation but upon fact.

* * *

12/February/2015 08:47 AM

If you are lying about what you did or didn't do, you are a liar.

If you are telling the truth about you and your actions, you are an honest person.

In the eyes of god and man which is preferred?

*   *   *

12/February/2015 08:46 AM

    If what you are doing is truly right there will be no one stepping forward to tell you that it is wrong.

* * *

12/February/2015 08:42 AM

If you are trying to hurt someone for what they did to you does that make you better or worse than them?

* * *

12/February/2015 08:41 AM

Do you think about other people first or do you think about yourself first?

First Hit Final Hit
12/February/2015 08:41 AM

Unfortunately, much of modern life is defined by conflict. People attempting to get ahead, people attempting to get over, people attempting to make themselves look good while making you look bad.

This being the case, one must forever learn ways to deflect and counter the attacks of others. For some this is entirely a mental game. It is about out maneuvering the other person, the individual you consider an opponent, to rise to the top of the heap.

Life lived at this level is very sad. It is not spiritual. It is not pure. It is not good. But, due to the large percentage of unconscious people who inhabit this life space, this is oftentimes the way it is.

The martial artist continually trains their body and their mind to defend and counter attack any type of attack that comes their direction. In some cases, no defense is the best defense. You simply let the false actions and misdirected movements of the opponent defeat themselves. Though this strategy takes time, it commonly expends the least amount of energy.

But, then there is the situation when the chokehold is executed. At this stage of the confrontation if one does not defend themselves they will be choked out and could die.

A side note, recently I met a person who had a distortion of their face. One that they did not have previously. How did it occur? A friend had put them in a chokehold and it had cut off essential blood flow. So, even in none aggressive situation, physical defense may be necessary.

The martial artist trains constantly to be able to defend themselves from all type of attacks. In the early stages of training this takes on the form of repetitive drills. As time progresses, however, the mind of the martial artist becomes focused and they begin to be able to expand their understanding to see and to deal with all types of physical onslaught. It is this mental training that allows them to see an attack before it is unleashed and to deal with any form of attack in the most expedient manner possible.

Those who desire to attack and dominate others set the actions of life in motion. But, life is truly actualized by those who understand how to control the aggression of the aggressor and debilitate them in the most subtle and expedient manner possible.

Excuses for Your Action
12/February/2015 08:37 AM

Have you hurt someone else by you doing what you do? If so, how many times? Is there a pattern in your life of doing things that damage the lives of other people? Do you feel that you have the right to do so? Do you believe you should be able to do whatever it is you want to do?

I believe if we step back we each see how wrong it is to hurt someone else. Yet, many people go throughout their life doing just that. They do what they do, they behavior in a manner that hurts or damages the lives of others and they never give it a second thought. They never give it a second thought until, in very rare instances, they are confronted with their actions and are forced to take a look at what they have done.

In many cases, the moment a person is confronted with their wrong actions or wrong behavior they go into the mode of, *"What? Did I do that?"* Or, *"I didn't know."* Perhaps most prominent is the person who denies all responsibility for their actions, to themselves, to the person they have wronged, and to their friends who will buy into their untruthful claims. In fact, the person with this type of personality will seek out people who they can turn to, who will listen to them, deny all responsibility for anything and in some cases turn the blame back on the person who was wronged.

Think about it. Have you encountered people like this? Are you one of these people?

No one is perfect in this world. We all do bad and wrong things either by accident or intent. But, if and when we do we should be adult enough, (for lack of a better term), to own what we have done, never do it again, and seek forgiveness by acknowledging our crimes and setting about to undo what we have done.

Few people are like this, however. Most run, hide, lie, and deny. If a person behaviors in this manner, what does that say about them? Are you one of these people?

Life is created by you and your actions. What are they?

The Land of Opportunity
12/February/2015 08:35 AM

I cannot tell you how many people I met all the time here in L.A. that come to this city to find fame and fortune. Young or old they believe that by coming here they are going to be able to live out their dreams. Wrong! Whether they are actors, directors, musicians, singers, artists, photographers, you name it, they are coming here to hit the big time. Not!

They all come out here and their dreams are smashed. I have known so many people, so full of faith and belief in themselves, but they all end up broke.

Some people come out here on family and money and take a bunch of acting classes. But, what do acting classes equal? Nothing. All they are is a way for the teacher to make a living by promising the dreamer a dream. If you're acting, you don't need acting classes. ...They are all a lie.

Some people come here to make films. A couple of people I know actually did make a low budget movie that was pretty good on their own will and their own dime. Good for them! I give them all respect because they are so few and few between. But, for most it is not like that. I have known more than a few who ended up bankrupt on believing that the movie they made would be a big hit. But, it was not.

I have written a number of times about actors and actresses who really thought they had the right stuff; the right look, the right attitude, and the talent. They believed that just because some person, someplace, sometime hit it big, so could they. Nope... It all equaled nothing.

It's like the ongoing joke about L.A., how the people you meet claim to be an actor but they are actually working as a waiter or waitress. That is pretty standard stuff.

If you want to come here and get a job-job, you can probably do that. Opportunities for standardized employment are mush greater in a big city than in a small town. But, if you are more than twenty-one years old, and are not beautiful, and willing to do whatever it takes, (if you know what I mean), to live your dream, forget it. It's all about who you know or who you blow. Hollywood only wants the young and the willing.

This is just a warning. A warning I've passed along for years upon years. Be prepared, L.A. is not what you think it is.

Coming Clean and the Less or More
12/February/2015 08:31 AM

Recently, at least here in the States, there has been all of this talk brought about by the fact that this one prominent newscaster was caught embellishing the truth. In fact, he has been suspended for six months from his network, while they launch an investigation, due to his words.

On networks like CNN and NPR there have been all of these talking heads discussing how people commonly embellish their memories to other people in order to make themselves sound bigger, better, or greater. They have also had memory experts on discussing how people's memories change over time and how some people produce false memories. All facts, and ideologies about truth and/or lies.

Do you lie? Have you ever embellished something about yourself to make yourself seem bigger or better? I believe that most people have. People do this knowing.

Have you ever been with a friend or a family member and they are telling a story that you were a part of but the story they tell is much greater and grander than it was when you lived it? Again, people tell their stories and they present them in the way they want others to hear them. True or false?

From a personal perspective, as someone with an eidetic memory, I remember everything. It is really a curse. I was probably in my forties before I realized that everyone doesn't remember everything with as much clarity as I do. I remember one girl telling me, *once upon a time,* a long time ago, *"I forget things pretty fast."* Meaning, she would forget her previous boyfriend in no time at all. ☺

Some people are like that. They live what they live, they

do what they do, but then the memory fades. It is gone.

In this modern world, and I am pretty sure it has been this way forever, people want to be seen as more. They want to be known as having lived death defying missions, and have returned to tell the story. They want to be seen as having done great things, made spectacular accomplishments. But, if the only thing they have done is lie about what they actually did, where does that leave them and all of those people who listen to their tall tales?

Words are just words. But, here is the problem – and this is where lying gets complicated... If someone tells another person a story about his or her life, and that person believes him or her, then that lie may get propagated to the world. The lie the person originally told is then told again and again and again by anyone who hears it and believes it. I believe this is where a lot of the world's religious mythology was born. But, here in life, all we have is our belief. All we have is what we hear and what we believe. But, if we are told a lie and we believe that lie, then what?

Sadly, due to this trend of deception in human behavior, this is why I never believe anyone until what he or she says can be proven. But, more than that... Have you ever met someone who has truly accomplished something in life? They are the most humble people. They don't brag. They don't tell stories about their achievements. They don't make up lies. They are silent in their accomplishments. This is because of the fact, (and I have said this over and over again), *"If you have truly accomplished something you don't have to tell anyone, because they will already know."*

These are the people I think we should all strive to be more like. Sure, go after whatever dream it is you may hold. But, don't lie about it. Just do what you do. If you accomplish something; great. If you don't; also great. But, never fall into the trap of believing that by telling a lie you actually are what you have falsely claimed you have achieved. Because you are not.

    A lie never equals the truth.

Defined By Circumstance
12/February/2015 08:24 AM

Have you ever met someone and you realize that if they had been presented with a better set of life opportunities every thing would have been different. This could be a person's socioeconomic standing, their religious ideologies, their race, their social environment, and the list goes on. But whatever it is, what made them what they are, they cannot run away from.

Most people only rise to the level of achievement that they are offered in life. Most people are defined by their family, their friends, and their social standing. Now, this is not always the case. Some people work hard, focus, and rise far beyond their contemporaries and their societal definitions. But, these people are few and far between. Most are trapped by circumstance.

I am sure I mentioned this man in writings of times gone past but his story ideally demonstrates what I am speaking of. When I was in high school I had this one friend who was one of those super smart people, everyone just knew he should go far. His father was a projectionist at a theater, which sounded pretty cool to us high school students. But, more than that, his father played the synthesizer, which was a new musical tool back then. The ethereal style of his music he created was a big influence to me. After high school my friend and I went our separate ways.

Several years later, I was in grad school, I was waiting for my evening seminars to begin so I went to see the newly re-released movie, Last Tango in Paris. When I was leaving, *"Scott... Scott... Is that you?"* There he was, my high school friend. He was actually the guy who took my ticket when I entered the theater but he had cut the very long hair he had in high school and I didn't recognize him. He had followed in his father's footsteps and was working at a movie theater. So smart... He should have done something big, but life and lack of money trapped him and kept him from going to college.

Me, I truly felt bad. Me, I was this wayward bohemian, bad student, and there he was this really intelligent guy trapped.

And, that is just one example. There are many more. I believe if we think about it we can each come up with an example.

The fact is, even the ability to get out of own way and move up is defined by our upbringing, our psychological mindset, and all the life things that make us who we are. We are what we are defined as long before we can ever create our own definition.

I believe this is why so many people, when they enter the later stages of their life, are so disappointed with whom they have become, or better put, have not become. They didn't have the tools to do what they truly wanted to do and, as such, got stuck doing only what was available.

No savior arrived, so no savior could be found.

Sometimes I meet people like this. Especially when they are young I can see all they can/should be; yet I also see what they will become. Now, this is not a judgment, for we are each defined by the who it is we are. Even though this is a defining factor of life, I think we each need to study the who and what we are, define it to the best of our ability, and then, while moving within that definition, rise to the best level of, "I," that we can be.

That's What Happens When You Hurt People
09/February/2015 07:54 PM

Kind of picking up on the blog I wrote earlier today... Have you ever noticed how when somebody has messed with other's people lives and then the shit starts coming their direction all they do is cry out with the, *"Whoa is me"* card... *"My life is so terrible. Could somebody please help me?"* And, so on...

Now, I think in most cases, when someone is down on their luck, we are each happy to reach out a helping hand. But, when that same person is known to have hurt or damaged our lives and/or the lives of others, sympathy is hard to find.

Moreover, this behavior is simply another projection of their own selfishness. ...The same selfishness that drove them into a state of desperation.

This is the thing to remember in life. We each do what we do. No matter what reasoning or justification we may have for doing what we did, it was we who did it. Thus, we are one hundred percent responsible for the consequences.

If you ever find yourself on the down side of karma, karma that you created, then instead of seeking the help of others, the better thing to do is to go out and do good things. First, repair any damage that you created. Then, move forward being selfless, not selfish, and do so many good things, for no good reason, that something good will finally come your way.

Nothing in life ever gets better unless you accept the responsibility for your actions and make things better. No crying out to people will ever help your situation if you do not stop your negative actions and fix what you have broken.

Good things come to those who do good things.

The Difference That You Make
09/February/2015 02:06 PM

Life is an interestingly complicated mess. People are torn between finding a way to make a livelihood, obtaining their desires, and for the few and the far between, finding a way to give back.

...Most people don't care. They are all about charting a pathway that allows them to have what they want and to live the lifestyle they desire and may whoever gets in their way be damned. Sad but true.

There are others, however. Those who want to give something back. They want to make the life of other people better and they may even want to make the entire world better. Though these are admirable and high sounding goals, how one obtains and achieving these goals is what comes to define any contribution a person may or may not make.

I think back several years ago to when I was asked to interview and write an article about modern martial art legend, Bill *Superfoot* Wallace. The reason I was asked to write the article was that there was some man falsely claiming to have obtained a black belt rank from him and was marketing himself using *Superfoot's* name. While we were talking Bill put something into words very profoundly. He said, in essence, *"A black belt used to really mean something. If someone had a black belt they really knew their stuff. If someone had a 2nd degree black belt, look out. Now, everyone is a 7th, 8th, and 9th degree and it means nothing."*

I believe there are many reasons a person becomes involved in the martial arts but I won't go into them here. But, I too remember when a black belt really meant something. Then, the shift came from Asian to Western instructors and the black belt began to be handed out all over the place. From this, what was even worse was the self-promotion that began to happen.

I think back to when I was in my last semester as an undergrad. My class on Urban Geography was going to Palmdale each weekend to map the businesses and home constructions, and interview some of the inhabitants, as Palmdale was growing very rapidly at that time. To put myself through school, I operated a martial art studio, so I was very well versed in the realms of the martial arts by that point in my life. While there, I came upon this one studio where the owner had tons of diplomas hanging on his wall. He was a black belt in pretty much every style there was. The funny thing was, at least to me, were all the diplomas were issued by the same organization. Okay... But, how can that be? Different styles equal different governing bodies.

Now, for anyone who knows anything about the martial arts, this is pretty much impossible; to have that many black belts in that many styles. Yet, there he was operating a studio. I am sure he had numerous students who believed whatever it was he was telling them. But, ultimately, by living that lie was he helping or hurting his students?

In term of spirituality, there are all kinds of people, who claim all kinds of things. Long ago I realized there was a lot of hypocrisy in spirituality and a lot of lying going on. There were so many fraudulent people, claiming so many things, that I almost couldn't believe it. At best, they were claiming the, *"Do as I say, not as I do,"* philosophy. At worst they were just flat out lying to people and deceiving them.

Maybe they honestly believed they were spiritual, I don't know? But, how can you pass on any form of true spirituality when your own soul is in torment and you are lying about who and what you are?

Are these people helping or hurting those who come to them for guidance? I believe the answer to that question is very obvious.

This is the thing... Some people may want to help. Even some fraudulent people may want to help. But, if a person is lying about who and what they are or if they have charted a false pathway to holding any credential they may claim, then anything they may give to others will be tainted by their own falsehood.

You really need to think about this before you go to study from anyone or to receive any type of anything from anybody: be it martial art training, spiritual guidance, or anything else. The question to forever ask is, *"What is their motivation for them doing what they are doing?"* And, *"Who are they and what credentials do they possess to be claiming to be a teacher, a spiritual guide, or anything else?" "Is what they are passing along of true, pure knowledge? Or, is it simply a way for them to stroke their own ego?"*

And. that is the ultimate question to pose to anyone who hopes to give anything, *"Why do you want to do it?"*

*   *   *

09/February/2015 12:45 PM

If you have an opinion about someone or something that means you are passing judgment.

If you present your opinion to other people that means you are being judgmental.

If you are being judgmental, what does that make you?

A person who claims to be an authority.

What makes you an authority on anything or anybody?

*   *   *

09/February/2015 08:20 AM

    People are only concerned with what is going on in your life when there is nothing important going on in their own.

Karma Unfolding
09/February/2015 07:39 AM

Recently, I bumped into a woman who, a couple of years ago, really messed with my financial stability. It would have been fine with me if I never saw her again but it seems that is not the way life is – whether you love or hate a person you are going to bump into them one more time after your time together is over.

Now, I won't bore you with the whys and the wherefores of what she did, just leave it to say she did what she did for absolutely no valid reason – the only reason was to create melodrama. And, that is exactly what occurred in my financial life for the better part of year and perhaps her actions flowed over even to the now as life builds upon what we have to work with.

Certainly, each of us has done things in our lives that have hurt other people. Most of us are not so cold as to do them intentionally, however, as this woman did to me. Moreover, if we do something wrong, that hurts someone; we feel guilty and do our best to try to remedy our wrong. This woman did none of that.

In any case, as I listened to her speak, she explained that she was now working at a fairly physically intensive job. "*I need money,*" she exclaimed. This, when she is now well into her retirement years. Due to me being who I am, I immediately felt compassion for her age and her situation. But, I could not also help but think about the karma that was taking place in her life. For if she had done what she had done to me, whom else had she taken a similar action towards?

But, as I sat there studying her life situation it made

think back to what I have been saying for a long-long time now, just because someone gets their karmic retribution for what they have done to you, that does not repair what they have done, nor does it make your life any better. Just as when a person goes to jail for their crimes, how does that repay the victims of those crimes in any manner?

I think it is important that we all look to the actions of our life and know why we do what do. It is probably impossible to not hurt someone in someway as we travel through life, but it is essential that we never set out to do this intentionally. We should only be thinking about how we can make each person's life better, not how we can harm them. And, if we have hurt someone, it is really essential that we take the initiative to remove, repair, and fix any damage that we may have unleashed.

Let's strive to make every person's life better, not worse.

The Damage That You Do
07/February/2015 09:53 AM

Of late, I've been writing a lot about and discussing, (with one of the university classes I teach), the subject of personal interactive patterns with the world; i.e. the helping hand you lend or the damage that you create. Realistically, I believe that we each have experienced patterns of both in our life. There have been times in our life that we have try to help someone or something and there have been times that we have done damage to people or things – whether intentionally or not. The biggest conclusion is that what we do, (whether knowing or not), and how we interact with life becomes a pattern. From this pattern we set about creating the entire destiny of the rest of our life.

In simple terms, if we help people, we are thanked and thought highly of – if we hurt people we are looked down upon. But, in life, (as seemingly is always the case), it gets a little tricky. For example, it seems that in life if you are doing critical and/or negative things you will always find a group of people to egg you on – give you support and cheer your negative words and deeds. Yes, if you do good things you will also find a group of supporters. But, due to the fact that there is rarely as much of an adrenalized undercurrent associated with doing good things, those people are commonly much more quiet in their praise. As such, the comradery appears to be less abundant.

It seems that bad deeds are done most frequently when a person is young. The reason for this is simply. If you are living under the roof of your parents, if your parents or family money supports you, then it appears that you will forever have a safety net; you are protected. Whatever you may do or whatever may happen from what you do, you will not have to suffer the brunt of the consequence. On the other hand, if you are totally self-supportive, then everything changes. If you must pay for and make your own way through the world, you become much more conscious of the fact that your actions have very specific, long reaching consequences, and if you walk down a path of embracing the negative you may end up in a very bad situation.

    Youth is where most people create the patterns of life interaction and the destiny for what they will become; be it good or bad. What you train your mind to do, how you learn to justify your actions, in your youth, is what will travel with you to adulthood. Now, I can say you should only say and do good things: don't hurt, don't steal, don't say or do bad things, but my saying it is of little motivation. Embracing a positive life is a conclusion that you must reach on your own if that is the path you hope to ultimately walk.

    Here again, we go back to the understanding that all patterns of our life are set forth in our youth. If you follow a path of focusing only on doing and saying positive and good things in your youth, this is where you will find yourself in adulthood. If, on the other hand, you get addicted to the rush of doing and saying negative things, cheered on by those around you who embellish the critical/negative mindset, then where will your life find you?

    Your life is your choice. But, it is essential to understand that what you say and what you do leads to your next set of available options. Even if you jump onto the negative bandwagon only for a moment that choice can set the entire stage for the rest of your life. Think about it...

* * *

07/February/2015 09:52 AM

Can doing something that hurts someone ever be considered a positive action?

Consciousness, Discretion, and What You Do With Your Life
06/February/2015 09:06 AM

I believe that each of us have encountered people that have made us wonder, *"What are they doing with their life?"* This may be a person who is doing illegal, immoral things; someone who is committing crimes, someone who is locked into a pattern of drug, alcohol, food, credit card, or tobacco abuse, or is hording, gambling, locked into sexual obsessions, and so on. Certainly, there are numerous Reality TV shows that have been devoted to people like this and movies that have been made about their actions, as well. Yes, these people have a problem and no matter what their psychological justification may be, (which is ultimately only an excuse), they should really get help and get their life right.

Some of these people catch themselves, take the steps to get on the right track, but many do not. Many are too lost in whatever mindset that they are embracing to ever change. What occurs from this is a life defined by the damage they cause to themselves and to others.

Though the above-mentioned conditions are very obvious to the onlooker, there are many more life patterns, that ultimately lead to a negative end, which are much more subtle. These are the ones that are embraced by a person who may seem to be very functional. They have a good education, a good job, an established relationship, and so on. Yet, what they are doing to themselves, to the people they interact with, and to this life space in general leads them down a pathway which only leaves a wake of damage, injury, and destruction.

It is very important to take a moment and take a long

hard look at yourself: study who you are, study who you associate with, study what are your desires and why, and study what impact you are having on the world around you by doing what you are doing.

Many people make excuses for all of their actions. *"I'm just making a living." "I hang around with this person because I have known them forever." "I associate with that person because I believe they need my help." "I do those things because they make me feel better."* And, the list goes on... But, if we step back and become very honest with ourselves it is very easy to see if what we are doing is good for us, good for those we associate with, and good for the world around us.

The problem is, most people never take the time to truly and honestly take a long hard look at themselves. What they do is to justify their actions or associate with people who will condone their actions. But, this is not living a life of consciousness. This is living a life defined by denial.

Ultimately, it is only you who can decide to live a positive life, creating as little damage to yourself, others, and the world as possible. Ultimately, it is only you who can step beyond the realm of justifications and become more. Ultimately, it is you who can choose to change.

If you want to live a life of consciousness and truly make the world a better place by your presence, the question you must forever be focused upon is *"What is what I am doing, doing to me, to others, and to the world?"* There is no right or wrong answer. But, I believe if we step back and remove all of the denial from our brain, we each will understand when we are doing something right or doing something wrong. Allow your inner being to be your guide and try to make all of your deeds conscious actions.

Make you better. Make the world better.

* * *

06/February/2015 08:14 AM

    Is what you are doing spreading a blanket of positivity onto the world or is what you are doing spreading a blanket of negativity onto the word?

    The answer to that question is easy. How do you feel? How do other people feel about you?

Doing Things To Piss You Off
06/February/2015 08:08 AM

There is a certain group of people who go about doing things to make people angry. This may be accomplished by talking behind their back, spreading false facts about them, straight out lying about them, or, as we have all heard about, attacking them via the various channels on the internet. Anyone who lives this lifestyle is embracing a very shallow and misdirected life. The moment you have to speak about someone/anyone else to make yourself feel relevant you are missing the entire point of life.

Life is about you living your life. Life is not about you saying things about others, talking about others behind their back, or throwing hidden jabs at others. If you have something to say about a person be man (or woman) enough to say it to their face. If you cannot do that, it means that you are afraid of what may happen to you, due to their reaction, and you are hiding behind a wall of fraudulent, insecure behavior.

People justify their words and their actions all the time. Their friends and their family may even tell them that what they are doing is okay. But, if you are not in direct contact with a person and you are saying anything negative about them, all that makes you is a coward.

Now, many people who inhabit the troll world of the internet will balk at that statement. If you are balking that means you are a troll. Direct contact is the only valid method of true interpersonal communication. If you are saying anything about a person, in any one way, that means that you are hoping you will never have to interact with the person of whom you speak as you are obviously afraid. Because if you weren't afraid, you would say it to their face.

Now, things don't always get physical in terms of when one person says something negative or questionable about another person to their face. We each have our own opinions. But, if you are not strong enough to speak your opinion directly to the person you have an opinion about, before you ever say anything about them to anyone else, that means you are hiding behind whatever veil of illusion you may be hiding behind. And, that is just wrong.

Think about how many of the world's problems have been created by people sneaking around behind the back of another person and spreading gossip about them. But, why do people do it? Are they jealous of that person? Are they envious? Are they scared? Or, have they simply developed a false opinion about a particular individual, fueled by what someone else said, who was also too afraid to confront them directly?

What is appropriate human interaction is a complicated questions and the answer is not easy to come by. What is for sure, however, is that true human interaction is based upon personal contact. You may love a person, you may hate a person, but if you are talking about anyone, in anyway without first discussion the subject with them personally, you are a life-fraud.

Words are a vicious tool. If you are going to use them at least be honorable enough to express your opinion in a face-to-face environment.

The Wrong of Right Language
06/February/2015 07:55 AM

Over the past week or so there has been a major uproar about NBC Newscaster Brian Williams fudging the truth about how a helicopter he was riding in taking RPG hits when it was, in fact, the helicopter ahead of him. Okay... Remember back in the Presidential election cycle of '08 when Hilary Clinton claimed she landed somewhere and bullets were whizzing past her head? Then she got busted on that fact and she fessed up it didn't really happen. Okay...

Everybody is in an uproar about Williams. But, let's think about a couple of things... First of all, who among us has not exaggerated some thing about our life experience and ourselves at some point in time? Who among us has not lied?

Like I always say... ...First it was in association with the filmmaking industry and now it is in association with all of life, *"Everybody lies."*

If you have never told a lie you are probably the only person on the planet who has not done so.

I'm not saying what Williams did was right. I am simply saying that this is life and that is what most people do.

Many of us, like myself, try not to behave in that manner. But, lying is rampant in this world. It is everywhere; everybody does it.

The thing that sets me to pondering is how and why everybody is so upset about this issue. Is it because they know they too have lied and would never want to be caught in their lie? Is it that they too have exaggerated and never want their exaggeration found out? Maybe if they focus is on someone else, the scrutiny will not go to them?

Mostly, what I have witnessed, more and more, is that people are angry at themselves, at life, at the world, at god, and/or at not living the life that they truly wish they could live so they become angry at whatever target they can find.

The question is, what is the truth? Is it the stories that you tell to the world and then they believe your words to be true? Or, is it what you have actually lived and only you know the true truth?

* * *

05/February/2015 02:59 PM

When you know a person is bad, when you know a person has bad intention and does bad things, it becomes your fault whenever that person does anything wrong. You make yourself responsible by continuing your relationship with that individual.

The Why of the Wonder
05/February/2015 02:48 PM

I was over on the Eastside today, blocking out some shots at this old warehouse where I'm about to shoot a music video. Afterwards, I was driving towards the freeway and I noticed a thrift store so I thought I would check it out. Didn't find much, just an old *Slick Rick* LP. But, what was more interesting is what I saw...

Inside, there was this girl, probably thirty-ish: Caucasian with long dark hair. For that area, Caucasian was a little different, but no big deal. More to the point is what she was wearing. She wore a very short mini skirt, very obvious fishnet stockings, and six-inch stiletto high heels. Now, that look would be all-good in a nightclub or something. But, this was mid-day in East L.A.

The guys in place, both young and old, were obviously checking her out. Me, that's not really my style. I'm more into the artsy girls who wear the long skirts with the big clunky shoes or combat boots. But, I am a heterosexual male, so when she bumped into me it did set a few thoughts and fantasies in motion.

But, the big question is why? Why was she dressed like that and hanging out in a thrift store in East L.A.? There could be a million explanations and I won't even try to venture a guess. But, like the people who dye their hair green or purple or wear really crazy clothing – what they want is to be noticed. No matter what their personal definition for why they want to be noticed may be, that is what they are seeking.

This girl, she got it. To what end, I know not. But, if nothing else she will be recorded in the *Akashic Records* for all eternity via this blog. Rock that look, baby. Rock that look... ☺

* * *

05/February/2015 09:24 AM

Change only happens when you change.

Distribution in the Digital Age
05/February/2015 08:39 AM

There is this one distribution company that I have been working with for years upon years. They have always been great. I can see my companies sales on a hourly basis so I know exactly what is going on – what movies are selling, what books are selling, and so on...

A couple of months ago my office staff began to receive emails from the company. As my people took mental note, they sent those mental notes over my direction.

What began to happen is that the staff at this distribution company was now answering questions posed to them by us five, six, seven, eight years ago. Very strange. I mean if the issue had still been an issue we would have recontacted them. And, maybe we did. But now, as I look back at these emails, I can remember the question or the issue but it is so far in the past that it does not even matter any more.

Why this is happening, I have no idea? And, it continues to happen. Don't the people at the company look at the date of the initial inquiries? I mean it's been years!

Overall, I find this whole thing very interesting. Interesting, to look at what was important back then and compare it to what is important in the here and the now. ...Times and desires and the need for specific information has moved on.

But, I don't know... Maybe it would be nice to go back five, six, seven, eight years and relive some of the what was done then so it could lead to a better now. And, maybe that is what the distribution company is doing, recharting the past.

Never mind, I'm getting way too metaphysical here... ☺

Reading into it What You Want
05/February/2015 07:55 AM

I forever find it interesting how people read a passage in a book and then put their own spin on the words. Two people read – two people have different takes. This is especially the case for those who read and interpret the so-called *Holy Scriptures*. Minsters read all kinds of their own meanings in biblical passages. They take a word here and a passage there and use it to present whatever point it is that they hope to make.

I don't know... It just seems a bit disingenuous. Just because the words are there (and this goes for any book) it does not mean that people should be able to reinterpret them and use them to their own advantage.

Anyway... There is a high profile minister, at an established predominately African-American church, here in L.A. Recently, in one of his sermons; he compared L.A.P.D. to the white hooded KKK. Yes, yes, there are always problems with people in a position of authority like the various police departments but it is simply wrong to compare the police to a mean-spirited group of individuals. For without law enforcement where would our society be?

I certainly understand this minsters motivation. As anyone who is my age or older (as this minster is) we can certainly look back to a time when racial profiling was a common occurrence and people were predominately defined by their race. And, a lot of bad things happened. I personally witnessed and experienced this. But, time has moved on.

I can tell you, as someone who has trained a lot of law enforcement professional in the martial arts, of all races, that there is very little racism going on in the L.A.P.D., the Los Angeles County Sheriffs Department, or any of the other police agencies I have worked with. What there is among law enforcement professionals is a commonality of distaste for those who unleash havoc on society and commit crimes either in gangs or as individuals. This is not defined by a person's race. It is defined by the type of person they choose to be and what they choose to do.

Yes, it is important to look back and learn from what has taken place in the past. From this, we can keep it from never happening again. But, it is also essential to not define this period of now by that past. We must keep moving forward and not let the past create our future.

Forgive and Forget
But What About When Neither One is an Option
04/February/2015 02:41 PM

I was discussing the concept of forgiveness with my class today. Now, this is a subject I have thought long and hard about and have written a few pieces on: both academically and personally.

The discussion began with, *"Why should someone be forgiven once they have done something wrong?"* The initial responses where the expected, *"Because it's the right thing to do." "It will make you feel better so you can move on,"* and so on... All canned responses broadcast to humanity from whom or where I know not.

Other students, however, were not so quick to react. ...Not so willing to say, *"Forgive and forget."*

I believe that many of us, perhaps those in the aforementioned group, have had something really bad done to them by a person, a group, a movement, or by life. I think that for someone who has experienced something very traumatic, orchestrated by the hands and actions of another, forgiveness does not come easy. And, I believe it should be that way.

Too often people are allowed to do something really wrong and then skate. They call up the forgiveness card either by asking for it from the person who was wronged or they claim, *"I'm sorry."* But, *"I'm sorry,"* means nothing. It's just words.

On the other side of the coin there are those who knowingly hurt others and not only do they not seek forgiveness for their actions but due to their psychological makeup they believe that they have done nothing wrong. Why should a person like that ever be forgiven?

The ultimate question is, *"Why?"* Why should anyone be forgiven for what they have done if they do not fix and/or undo what they have done?

This is a theme I continually go back to in my writings. If you do something, you did it. You need to be responsible for your actions and either bask in the benefits or suffer the consequences. It is you who did it, who else should feel the karma?

Though, as expected, there was no ultimate conclusion reached by my class, what most came to understand was that each situation and each person is defined by their own set of parameters. As such, those who have lead a fairly unhindered, undamaged life need not simply dish out the canned philosophy of, *"Forgive and forget."* Because the truth be told, when you have been hurt by the actions of another, forgiveness is only a game of pretend, because you can't forgive as forgetting is near impossible.

*   *   *

04/February/2015 09:55 AM

Do you take action about your inaction?

* * *

04/February/2015 09:54 AM

Your life is defined by who surrounds you.

* * *

04/February/2015 09:53 AM

When you are alone, whom can you fight with?

*   *   *

04/February/2015 09:52 AM

If there is no god who can you blame when things go wrong?

Patterns of Peculiarity
04/February/2015 09:52 AM

Life is defined by a system of patterns. All of life and all of nature follows a constant. All of existence flows until catastrophe strikes: be it an earthquake, intense weather, famine, or something man made like war or a nuclear meltdown.

People too follow patterns. If a person goes to school or has a job they must rise at a certain time, prepare themselves, and arrive at a prescribed time ready to do what is expected of them.

This is all natural. There is, however, another level of patterns brought about by a specific person.

Have you ever seen a person who goes to the same restaurant, day in and day out, and they must sit at the same seat? To them, that is their desire. To everyone else they are just seen as weird and invasive.

A restaurant is just one example. People obsess about all kinds of things and actions they believe they must make/take. But, it is all in their head. It is all based upon their misplaced desires. They do things in an exacting manner. They leave at the same time, arrive at the same time, do the same thing, day in and day out.

By living life in this format, a person forms unnatural patterns based upon obsessive consciousness. The more they do it, they more they believe they must do it. Some even fight to do it.

This type of behavior is against the patterns of nature, however, and it sets the person constantly at odds; not only with themselves – because they strive to do what only they believe it is they must do but with others, as well, for their insane necessity to do all things in a certain way, at a certain time, sets them against those other people who must interact with them.

Change and difference is necessary. It is the natural pattern of life. Just as nature erupts when something has become too common, so too should each person. For with difference, things become different. From this new levels of human experience and new realizations are found.

Do something new.

Some People Do Bad Things
04/February/2015 09.51 AM

It is no secret that one of my most pervasive pastimes is to go to Flea Markets, Swap Meets, Antique Stores, and Thrift Shops. You never know what you are going to find and sometimes, every now and then, you discover something very-very cool.

As one of my most pervasive diversions, (when I have the time), is to go to Thrift Shops, I sometimes get to know the people that work at them. My lady always tells me I need a better set of friends. But, I'm down with the down, okay... I like people on all levels of life.

Anyway, I went into a thrift store and one of my thrift store buddies greeted me. I asked how she was. She was upset. Somebody had apparently brought in a piece of luggage full of shit and when she opened it to see what was inside, some of it got on her hand. She was mad. I would be mighty pissed off too.

Why would somebody do something like that? I can only imagine... But, it was probably because they were mad at the store.

Now, people get mad at people, stores, and life situations all the time. But, it is how you react to that anger that defines who and what you are. The fact is, if you go to an animalistic level, what does that make you? An animal. There is nothing cool or righteous about living your life on that level.

I believe in life we have each become angry at someone or something. That's very normal. But, how we react to that sets the next course of our life in motion. Look at the rap mogul who last week got pissed off, ran over and killed one person and injured another. Immediately, he was caught and is now in jail. That's what uncontrolled anger can lead to.

...If you do bad things you may go to jail. ...If you kick a person's ass that you are mad at you may go to jail. But why do any of that? Why let the person or the situation, that has made you angry, defines the next set of actions in your life?

From a personal perspective, I think back a few years ago to how this one person, (very eloquently, I must add), was presenting a group of falsehoods about me to the world via the internet. People being who people are then ran with them using it as a reason to become angry at me. ...Me, who had done nothing. None-the-less, I was the focus of their rage. Personally, I was amused by what this person had said about me and about the way people were reacting but that is just who I am. But, I could also see the damage that it was causing. Those inflicting the damage did not care, however.

Creating damage on any level is simply wrong. Doing damage to anyone or anything, on any level, for whatever reason, never makes anything right.

At one point, during this period, I received this raging email from this one guy cursing me every direction; all to hell. But, his anger was completely misplaced. He didn't even know the facts. He went on to write a very well-written piece about my supposed actions and his opinion about me and posted it on a website. The thing was, it was all based upon speculation and it was completely false. Though he used his real name on the website, he used a false name in the email. By now, people should know that it is very easy to trace the source of an email and they were both by him: the article and the email. Again, I found it very amusing. But, I also saw the damage it caused.

You know, the sad thing was, the aforementioned emailer/author often speaks of his possessing Asperger syndrome in his articles and his posts. Me, I have spent a good percent of time helping those with Asperger, particular through the martial arts, as well as writing about those with Asperger who have suffered at the hands of other due to their possessing this condition for several magazines. But, I am sure the guy never knew that. He never researched me. He just based his appraisal upon what someone else had said and then moved forward motivated by misplaced emotion. Thus, all that continued to be unleashed, from the initial person's action forward, was damage.

The point being, what you do is what you do. What you do sets a whole avalanche of new life events in motion. Most people believe that if they are doing something to someone else and that person suffers because of it they will be left immune from any consequences. But, this is never the case. All we do is all we do. If it affects anyone else, it also affects us. That is why we each should only perform conscious, helping actions – speak only conscious, kind words.

It is like my rude neighbor who I have spoken about in the past. Here's a guy who is claiming to be some sort of spiritual conduit and actually charging for his service. That is bad in and of itself. But then, he totally destroyed the vibes of our community when he moved into it by doing things like talking insanely loud, preaching his form of regurgitated gospel out the windows, and perpetually screaming, *"Fuck me,"* at the top of his lungs whenever he was upset. All this while telling people, who didn't know him in-person, that he was spiritual. But, for all of us who were left interacting with his actions we knew that statement was very false.

If that had been me, doing what he had done, I would be so embarrassed that I would never show my face in the area again and instantly move away. But, he hasn't done that. I don't know... Maybe my writing about him is his only claim to fame?

In any case, I have to question, how do you behave in that manner and not be totally ashamed of yourself? Not to mention how can you claim to be a spiritual anything and be that out of tune with your surroundings and that out of control of your emotions?

And, this is the thing; people do bad things based upon their emotions. Some do them consciously while others do them unconsciously but, none-the-less, they are done. The truth be told, doing anything bad, no matter how emotionally driven you are, never ends in the betterment of anything. Bad only equals bad. Negative only equals negative. It is for this reason, even if you are angry, as we all become, it is better to take positive action to set things right, than to deliver a suitcase full of shit to a facility where the people who work there are not responsible, in any way, for your anger.

Put a Little Bit of Lie On It
04/February/2015 09:50 AM

Have you ever listened to a person tell a story? A story about something you lived with them. Do you ever notice how the story is not the way you remember it or maybe you actualize realize it is an exaggeration from the way you live it?

People lie. People put, *"A little bit of lie on it,"* as I like to jokingly define it. But, why is that? Why do people want to make a life moment lived appear to be bigger than it actually was?

I suppose there are a million reason but they all point to one thing, people lie. People want to appear to be more than they are, they want to actually be more than they actually are, and they want to have lived more than they have actually lived.

At the root of life is our life: what we have done, whom we have interacted with, and what we have accomplished. Within our inner being we know the truth about all that has and has not taken place. Many wish to alter that truth, however. Do you? If you do, you are not only living a lie but you are creating a lie. Moreover you are perpetuating the lying nature of all of humanity. One lie leads to the next and to the next and to the next.

Who are you? Do you lie? If you do, look deeply into yourself and define your reason why. Then, stop it!

A lie never makes the truth more true.

Saying Everything That I Said
04/February/2015 09:50 AM

It is always amusing for me to listen to a person speaking, read the writings of a person, or the words that are spoken when an individual is being interviewed and they say exactly what I have already said but they claim it as their own ideology. It is strange... It is flattering, (I guess)... But, it is also a bit disconcerting...

In fact, there have been a few people who while attempting to rip on me have actually stolen a passage I have written; word for word and have used it as if they invented it. I mean, if you are going to be critical at least think up your own things to say. ☺

But, let's get more to the point... If you are writing something that means you have something that you feel needs to be said. If you are being asked questions in an interview that means you have done something/accomplished something that others find worthwhile. All good...

The fact is, if you have done something worth doing you must first have a philosophy to guide you towards doing it. Most people have none. Thus, when they try to do something they fail at it miserably. No philosophy equals no true expression of that philosophy. Thus, nothing can be created.

Okay... But, where did that philosophy come from?

We each are influenced by our time in history, other people, and the world around us. For those of us who have a creative mission in life, we do things that create an end result – an object, a thought, or a thing. Then, when we are asked how or why it is we, the creative proponent of that equation, created what we did, we must come up with an explainable logic that guided us to create our creation and how others may follow in our path if they hope to do something similar.

Certainly, I have written a lot about a lot of stuff. I have spelled out my, *"Why and How,"* for all that I do. I do that to help others overcome obstacles if they hope to follow a similar path. But, for those who take the understandings and philosophies that I bottled and then call it their own – I don't know? It is perplexing...

I think back to when my *Zen Filmmaking* buddy Donald G. Jackson was still alive and when we were interviewed, either as a team or as a separate entity, our answers were often times very similar. That was because we had created a movement together, *Zen Filmmaking.* We didn't base it on anything that had been done before. We based it on our own understanding of the NOW and the creativity of immediate inspiration; leading to cinematic enlightenment. Without our interaction Zen Filmmaking would never have happened. Yes, I was more literate on the subject and more focused on formalizing and presenting *Zen Filmmaking* definition to the world, but without our teaming up, it may never have been an actualized entity. So, when we said the same thing, it was expected. But, when others say what I have said, sometimes exactly – write what I have written, and don't throw me a bone, it is very surprising...

Like I have always said about *Zen Filmmaking,* *"Make it your own."* You don't have to do what I do, just do it. Remove as many obstacles as you can and do what works for you. But, I think I should also probably paraphrase here, if you are going to quote me, use my words and my philosophies, say what I have already said, at least throw me a bone and state where your words and/or your ideology came from.

Distractions and Abstraction
04/February/2015 09:49 AM

We each find our own means to step back and live life on the level we want to live life. Me, I spent most of my adult years constantly returning to Asia. Every time for any reason, I would go. Finally, a couple of years ago I made my self stop doing that as my distraction. I realized that I had so much material I had created in Asia: photographs, art, words, music, films, that I really needed to get it organized and out there or it may all go to waste. So, I stopped going all the time. Instead, I got to get the doing done. And, it was a good thing.

How we find our distractions is what comes to define each of our lives. What we do equals what we have done. When you look forward there is the forever of all you want and hope to do. When you look back there is all that you should have done. But, in that equitation is the variable of what you have done while you were doing what you were doing. This is where life gets complicated.

If you spend your time getting high or drunk what have you accomplished? If you spend your time gaming or watching TV what have you lived? If you spend your time playing the game of lies and deceit, what are you left with? If you spent your time in the mode of acquisition, when you have what you wanted then all you want is something more. All of these things lead to living an unfulfilled life.

In our seeking of distractions, (and we all need them), we must find a conscious balance between the what soothes our being and what we leave to the world.

Whatever you do sets the next everything in motion in your life. Thus, whatever you do must be done from a mindset of consciousness.

The Blog is Back
04/February/2015 09:48 AM

Okay everyone... Here we go again. A New episode of the Scott Shaw Zen Blog.

Scott Shaw Books-in-Print:

About Peace: A 108 Ways to Be At Peace When Things Are Out of Control

Advanced Taekwondo

Arc Left from Istanbul

Ballet for a Funeral

Bangkok and the Nights of Drunken Stupor

Bangkok: Beyond the Buddha

Bus Ride(s)

Cairo: Before the Aftermath

Cambodian Refugees in Long Beach, California: The Definitive Study

Chi Kung For Beginners

China Deep

Echoes from Hell

Essence: The Zen of Everything

e.q.

Guangzhou: A Photographic Exploration

Hapkido: Articles on Self-Defense: Volume 1

Hapkido: Articles on Self-Defense: Volume 2

Hapkido: Essays on Self-Defense

Hapkido: The Korean Art of Self-Defense

Hong Kong: Out of Focus

Independent Filmmaking: Secrets of the Craft

In the Foreboding Shadows of Holiness

Israel in the Oblique

Junk: The Backstreets of Bangkok

Last Will and Testament According to the
    Divine Rites of the Drug Cocaine

L.A. Street Shots: A Photographic Exploration

L.A.: Tales from the Suburban Side of Hell

Los Angeles Skidrow: 1983

Marguerite Duras and Charles Bukowski:
    The Yin and Yang of Modern Erotic Literature

Mastering Health: The A to Z of Chi Kung

Nirvana in a Nutshell

One Word Meditations

On the Hard Edge of Hollywood

Pagan, Burma: Shadows of the Stupa

Sake' in a Glass, Sushi with Your Fingers: Fifteen Minutes in Tokyo

Scream of the Buddha

Scream: Southeast Asia and the Dream

Scribbles on the Restroom Wall

Samurai Zen

Sedona: Realm of the Vortex

Shama Baba

Shanghai Whispers Shanghai Screams

Shattered Thoughts

Singaore: Off Center

South Korea in a Blur

Suicide Slowly

Taekwondo Basics

Ten to Thirty

The Chronicles: Zen Ramblings from the Internet

The Ki Process: Korean Secrets for Cultivating Dynamic Energy

The Little Book of Yoga Breathing

The Little Book of Zen Mediation

The Lyrics

The Most Beautiful Woman in Shanghai

The Passionate Kiss of Illusion

The Screenplays

The Tao of Chi

The Tao of Self Defense

The Voodoo Buddha

The Warrior is Silent: Martial Arts and the Spiritual Path

Zen Mind Life Thoughts

The Zen of Life, Lies, and Aberrant Reality

The Zen of Modern Life and the Reality of Reality
TKO: Lost Nights in Tokyo
Urban India: Bombay, Delhi, Lucknow
Varanasi and Bodhi Gaya: Shade of the Bodhi Tree
Wet Dreams and Placid Silence
Woods in the Wind
Yoga: A Spiritual Guidebook
Yosemite: End of the Winter
Zen and Modern Consciousness
Zen Buddhism: The Pathway to Nirvana
Zen Filmmaking
Zen in the Blink of an Eye
Zen Mind Life Thought
Zen O'clock: Time to Be
Zen: Tales from the Journey
Zero One

www.ingramcontent.com/pod-product-compliance
Lightning Source LLC
Chambersburg PA
CBHW081830170426
43199CB00017B/2693